Warm wishes –

Brenda Knight Graham

Best Wishes

Jim Fellows

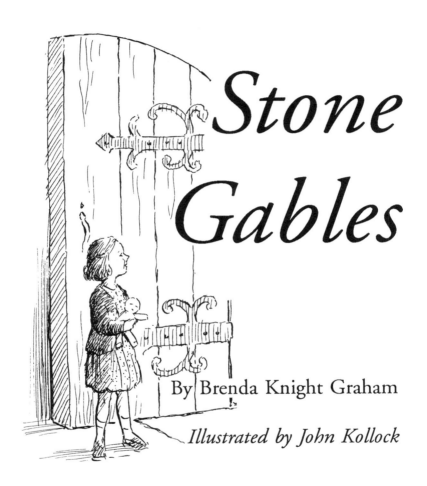

Stone Gables

By Brenda Knight Graham

Illustrated by John Kollock

Pilot Books
P. O. Box 941
Athens, Georgia 30603

Dewey Decimal Classification: 301.42
Subject heading: FAMILY
Library of Congress Catalog Card Number: 78-52615

Printed in the United States of America

To Mamma
with love

"He that dwelleth in the secret place of the most High shall abide under the shadow of the Almighty. I will say of the Lord, He is my refuge and my fortress: my God; in him will I trust."

Psalm 91:1 – 2, KJV

Contents

Foreword 9

Acknowledgements 10

1. Windows and Chimneys 11

2. Company Call 22

3. The Season of...Spring 37

4. The Season of...Summer 62

5. The Season of...Fall 84

6. The Season of...Winter 120

7. Mystery Unveiled 142

8. Our Honeymooners 157

9. Paid in Full 177

10. Mamma and Daddy Go Traveling 182

11. Can they See the Same Moon? 192

12. From Wicks to Switches 202

13. Where There Abideth Faith... 207

HILLS OF GEORGIA

Across the land, across the sea
The hills of home are calling me—
Red hills, green hills, far blue hills
    of Georgia;
Gray hills, misty, sun-kissed hills
    of Georgia.

Across the land, across the sea,
My dear hills are calling me—
Dear red hills, rocky old hills,
    time worn hills of Georgia.
Apple grown hills, sunset hills,
    pine clad hills of Georgia.

Across the land, across the sea,
The hills of home are calling me.

—F. S. Knight

Foreword

I first came to know Brenda Knight Graham when she began writing little essays in our local weekly paper *The Tri-County Advertiser*. At the time she was a high school student, but the images she evoked showed a depth of appreciation of God's world which I still treasure. Over the years I have come to know Brenda and her family. They are an amazing collection of talented people who have found their way in the world as missionaries, teachers, writers, and solid citizens of their communities.

Although I never had the pleasure of knowing the father of the family, I have treasured the visits I have had with Mrs. Floyd S. Knight who is now in her ninetieth year. She and her home, Stone Gables—the manor house which her husband created by hand—are the heart of the Knights' world. Here through the lean years of the Depression and with the uncertain income of a fine artist, the Knights home schooled their large family and gave them a sense of values that is evident several generations later.

We hear a lot today about parents wanting to give their children everything. This is usually expressed in clothes, cars, games and "things." What the Knights gave their children was a love of God and family; a sense of honor and honesty; an appreciation of natural beauty in nature and the joy of finding it for themselves. In doing this they truly gave their children everything they needed to have a rich full life.

In this book of that growing up time, Brenda has captured the feeling of everyday life at Stone Gables. I continue to enjoy and appreciate her gifts as a writer, and am honored to have a small part in helping to illuminate some of the imagery.

John Kollock
Clarkesville, Georgia
September, 1994

Acknowledgements

Writing *Stone Gables* in the seventies was a journey home. Re-editing it in 1994 has been another trip along a dear familiar road. Some curves were sprinkled with tears, others wound between hills echoing with happy laughter. I am so grateful to the following who took this walk with me: my husband, Charles W. Graham; my mother, Eula G. Knight; my nine brothers and sisters who, each in his/her own way, gave constructive criticism and encouragement; John Kollock, illustrator, critic, friend; Dawn Stanford, marvelous typist; Harley and Debi Rollins for their sound Christian counsel; and Audrey Roberson, faithful prayer. Lastly, a large warm thank you goes to all those readers who asked where they might find copies of *Stone Gables*. I count you as my friends.

Brenda Knight Graham
Cairo, Georgia

Chapter One
Windows and Chimneys

The sunshine made a lot of difference in the colors of Stone Gables house. The early morning sunlight slanting from the east through the crabapple and juniper made the windows look like twinkling fires, and the gray slate roof turned warm under its touch. Sometimes a tiny mist would rise from the roof as it warmed. You couldn't see much of the stonework at the back of the house because of a profusion of lime bushes planted close to the walls where ivy also climbed. But where flint stones did shine through foliage they appeared damp and glisteny.

Later in the day the southern part of the house was washed in white light and the stones around the French doors and overhanging oriel window looked warm in their soft colors of faintest orange, bluish pink, and white. The great elm and bushy juniper at the corner near Daddy's study kept his windows in shadow nearly all day. Ivy climbed the south chimney and worked its way around the windows, clutching the stones with little clawlike roots. Ivy leaves glistened in a liquid shine when sunlight found them. There were shifting patches of light on our flagstone patio and its wide wall where we often sat for terrace picnics. The house literally hugged a large oak tree which had flagstones over its roots. Sometimes a cat used that tree for a quick escape to the roof. We had a reputation for living in a house with a tree inside, but it would be more realistic to say it was a house snugged smack against an oak.

Afternoon sun finally found the front and western side of the house with its four sets of three windows each and its wide stone steps leading to thick oak double doors. All morning those doors looked almost black; the steps were cool in shadows, and windows looked out shadily through hanging clumps of ivy. But when sunshine swept around, the grayness and cold whiteness turned to warm pink and orange. The doors took on a welcoming luster, the great, round, iron knocker seeming to smile. If you came walking up the hill in the evening, perhaps with a pail of cold spring water sloshing against your skirt, you would see what appeared to be a hundred tiny sunsets gleaming from the leaded windows. The stonework was rosy, too, and in places light even danced on the gray slates.

The north end of Stone Gables with the largest of the house's three chimneys was eternally in shadow. The chimney itself reached up into sunlight. But down behind the hedges, under low windows, encouraged by damp shade, little ferns and mosses always grew.

Sunlight affected the interior, too. After breakfast, while a kettle hummed on the iron stove, a bar of sunlight found its way through a corridor window and the little narrow kitchen window to lie cozily across the small wood table where Mamma stacked dishes to drain. It also touched a favorite chair by the open stove grate where a cat usually purred in a comfortable curl. Only at a certain time in the afternoon did sunshine come through a little, translucent, arched window on the stairway and seek out the darker side of the kitchen. There were the open shelves with cookbooks, spices, and counter-like bin lids that hid supplies of ground meal, wheat flour, and brown sugar. When the sunlight came, it was like an evening blessing. Pat, oldest of us girls, liked to think that stream of sunshine was God looking in, and she tried her best to have every pot and pan in place, dishpan hung on its nail, bin covers clean and gleaming by the time it shone in. It was sort of a game she played with God.

The study, where Daddy stayed most of the time, was always dark. It had to be that way because the light hurt his eyes and made his head ache. He had had two sunstrokes while homesteading in Florida and waiting for Mamma to grow up so he could marry her. Now, we younger ones particularly, only knew him to avoid the sunshine religiously. If for some reason he had to be exposed, he carried a piece of cardboard to shield his head, and he always wore his rounded gray pith helmet like the ones elephant hunters wear in Africa. Even the Hall was very shadowy on Daddy's account. But that meant it was always cool, even in long hot stretches of August. Some sunlight found its way through thick ivy and lay across green and gray floor slates in fascinating patterns, but not very much.

The Hall was a very large room reaching the length of the house with fireplaces in each end, open beams above as far as the second story went, cathedral ceiling where an open staircase framed the parlor area with balconies. Sunlight shone through upstairs leaded windows and cast lace arched shadows across glistening stair rail and gray walls.

Upstairs it was sunny and airy. I was glad when Mamma and Daddy moved a large oak bench from the Hall to a wonderful spot beneath three windows on the top-stair landing. Stretched out there on my stomach with a book, sunshine embracing me, I could travel to England, go back to pioneer days, ride into the sunset following the west, and climb the Swiss Alps, breathing in sharp thin air with Heidi.

There were two places upstairs where sunshine never came directly. One was the Little Room, a tiny attic room opening into the east bedroom, really only a closet. One end of it was used for storage, but the other end made a delightful playhouse, at least Suzanne and I thought so. She was youngest and I next to youngest of Mamma's and Daddy's eleven offspring. We kept that playhouse strewn with our playful creations: a matchbox chest of drawers, for example, an oatmeal box cradle, and a thousand Sears catalog paper dolls.

It was light in the Little Room in the mornings because the east room would be filled with sunlight and would reflect it into the farthest corner of our playhouse where the roof tapered to the floor. Of course only in summertime could we play in the mornings and then only if we were lucky enough not to be put on cow watching duty or weeding detail. Afternoons were shady, but very cozy, the warmth from Daddy's study fire rising on chilly days.

The Little Room was a great place to eavesdrop because of being immediately above Daddy's study. We could lie stomach down, ear down, and listen to the conversations below. It was a very popular place for all four of us youngest ones during the month of November when Mamma and Daddy ordered our Christmas presents from catalogs. If one of us made the least little creak, though, Daddy would say loudly to Mamma, "Eula, I do believe there are rats up there," and items to be ordered dulled to shoes and work shirts.

The other place where sunshine never reached was the big closet. It was a very good place to hide when playing hide-and-go-seek on rainy days. There were big winter coats to scrunch behind or boxes of outgrown clothes or, best of all, Grandfather Knight's big steel-rimmed trunk. But at night it was a place to avoid. The glow of a kerosene lamp strategically placed on the balcony did not help dispel the terrors of those same winter coats transformed into horrible ghosts. The worst part about the closet was the Black Horn. We younger children had been made to believe by older ones that the Black Horn could rise up by itself from the top of the trunk and bleat out its awful sound like the worst kind of fog horn. It was an unexplainably horrible sensation knowing that inanimate, very dismal, object could come alive and take on character. It was understood we could never tell any adult of our fears, for then if the horn should ever "catch" us alone, it would certainly punish us. The form of punishment wasn't known, but could be imagined. This hideous thing was really only the harmless, horn-shaped part of an old Victrola. But I went to sleep many a night with covers pulled up over my head, my whole body sweating, comforted only by the distant sound of Mamma's voice reading to Daddy and to the children old enough to "stay up."

Stone Gables wasn't the only house at Pinedale. Down the spring vista you could see a small pine house with gray shingles. It had served as Daddy's studio when he was an active artist and even now was still called the Studio. Across a years-worn path from the Studio was a quaint cottage used as a guest house, laundry, and storage for spinning wheels and other fascinating relics. The two houses looked at each other in a friendly way across a path ambling between a lilac bush and a thick bed of ground myrtle.

The Studio was the older of the two. It was the house Grandfather Knight built when he first settled near Clarkesville, Georgia, in 1888, having come all the way from Michigan hunting the right climate for Grandmother who had tuberculosis. The house was cozily set not far from a spring, mothered by a giant poplar tree.

The family fell in love with those original five acres of piney land. The family in 1888 included Grandfather and Grandmother, her mother and sister, Daddy, who was two when they first moved to Georgia, and later his little adopted sister Hazel. Grandfather built the cottage so there would be room for everybody. The Studio had only two rooms.

Even though Grandfather had to go farther south trying to find the right climate for Grandmother, they came back to Pine-

dale at her insistence. Daddy was only thirteen when she died. He used to talk to us a lot about how pretty and delicate she was. Her grave was in a tiny stone-walled graveyard at the end of a pine-shaded path. There were lots of ferns and lilies of the valley around the graves and the wind always seemed to whisper high in the pines. If you had to be buried, this graveyard was a very nice place.

We children loved to play around the little houses. Actually, when I say "we children," I'm usually referring to the four youngest: Stanley, Charles, Brenda, and Suzanne. The oldest ones of our eleven were born and lived several years in the cottage before Stone Gables was built, and the middle ones of our clan had their own times playing on the mossy steps and around the lilac bush, I'm sure. We four, the "bottom rungs," the "little boys" and "little girls," were a family within a family, very much connected to the wonderful "older ones," yet with unique relationships all our own.

Sometimes we pretended we were Mamma and Daddy when they were courting. One of our favorite scenes was of Daddy painting Mamma's portrait. Mamma was only fifteen and Daddy thirty-three at the time so painting her portrait was the only way he could get permission to be with her. Even then he was so surrounded by chaperones that he couldn't say much to her, mostly just look and think, I guess.

I was glad when I could pretend to be Mamma with her long, golden hair and blue eyes. I'd climb the cottage steps, being ever so graceful leaning on Charles's arm (if he didn't jerk me) as he played the role of Mamma's brother. Stanley, who was playing Daddy's part, would meet us at the door, and we'd just touch hands before Suzanne, as Daddy's spinster aunt Dee, came pouncing on us, "Now, they must be hot from their long train trip. They must have something to drink before you start. Really, Floyd, why you make this child come all the way from Cornelia...You know you could find a subject just as good closer to home."

It was fun to rummage in an old chest that contained little, yellow cloth tobacco bags with tiny drawstrings, ancient petticoats, a musty, mothy black dress, and a lot of other musty, mothy things. We found enough apparel to dress up in and have the wedding on the cottage's side porch.

Charles was always the preacher, partly because his name was Charles (same as Mamma's brother who had married them in the Gibbs's L-shaped farmhouse), partly just because he was a good preacher. He did good squirrel funerals, too. Stanley was always Daddy, and Suzanne and I took turns being Mamma or her mother, Grandma Gibbs. We never had an actress to do Aunt Dee at the wedding. Whoever was Grandma always cried into a handkerchief and said, "My little girl, my baby!" But at the end Grandma would dry her eyes and kiss her new son-in-law on the cheek. Well, actually the play only went that far a time or two. Often the boys leaped off the porch mid-scene and were off to the brook, a tall tree, or a deep dark cave leaving "bride" and "Grandma" to play dolls or forage for ripe persimmons.

Mamma and Daddy had four children when they moved into Stone Gables. Orman was born in the studio, Pat and Brantley in the cottage. But John was born in the cabin far away in the woods Daddy had by then acquired. That cabin would later be our own private schoolhouse. Mamma asked Daddy please to let her have that fourth baby in the woods where she could have some peace and quiet while Aunt Dee ran the cottage household. Daddy agreed before he knew he'd be serving on the jury right at her time of confinement. He and Orman took her meals, checked on her often, but allowed her that treasured "peace and quiet." I think it was the last she had for a very long time.

John always liked to brag about being like Abe Lincoln who was also born in a log cabin.

The house wasn't finished when Daddy moved his family in. There wasn't a banister along the stairs; in fact, at first there weren't even any stairs, just a ladder. Daddy would stand at the bottom of the ladder in the morning and call out his children's names, and as each heard his/her name their feet hit the floor. Orman and Pat have wonderful memories of helping finish the big stone house, Brantley, too. Mamma's stories of life before house completion aren't quite as glowing.

From Ginger down we were all born in Stone Gables, several of us in the walnut bed with the high posts that had grapes and leaves carved on them. Carol, our sister whom I never saw, was born there, too. She was almost four years old when she got sick and died. I used to wonder a lot whether she were still four in heaven or if she were getting older like us.

Pinedale was a place where trees grew tall and wild animals wandered freely. We even heard a wildcat screaming in the meadow one night. I stood at the east room's oriel windows thrown open to the south and shivered at the eerie sound. Pinedale was Daddy's dream come true, a place where ten children could grow up in close communion with nature. There was always a tree to hide behind if one's feelings were terribly hurt. There was room for each of us to have a secret hiding place, and there were enough of us that we could always find someone with whom to share a secret. And there were always a lot of secrets to discover! Pinedale, Stone Gables, Home—the place where people cared about you just as you were.

Chapter Two

Company Call

Swoosh! Plop. Swoosh! Plop. It wasn't a very long slide, but it was fast and slick. We had taken off all but our underwear so the red clay wouldn't ruin our clothes and so we could be freer going down the bank. Fortunately, this marvelous spot on the side of a hill wasn't far from Ramble Brook. When our slide got a little dry and slow, we made oak-leaf cups and dipped them full of water which we poured down the slide to slicken it again.

A nice exposed root at the top of the slide made a fine launching place. At the bottom the slider came to a splattery halt in soft gooshy mud. When you pulled yourself up, it made a squishy noise. One afternoon four of us were using the bank which made for a busy slide.

We four were the only ones of our family still young enough to play in Pinedale's 150 acres of playground. Stanley, the oldest of our foursome, was fourteen and long-legged, too big to get much of a thrill out of the red bank. Other activities on our north Georgia pine-forested, hilly home place would be more to his liking, such as carving an Indian boat, building a dam, or climbing a look-out pine. But he was a good sport and seemed to have a good time sliding and splattering.

Stanley ran his fingers through his almost kinky shock of brown hair, forgetting about the mud on his hands. "Guess we better get under the falls and wash up," he said as he felt a trickle down his cheek.

Charles, eleven, squinted at the western sun beginning to drop behind the ridge. "Shucks! I reckon so," he agreed. His hair, bleached almost blonde from the summer sun, was the easier of the two boys for Mamma to keep trimmed neatly with her hair cutting set. He did have a cowlick at the back that stood out and

quivered if he were angry or nervous. But his hair didn't tangle and snarl like Stanley's.

We reluctantly gave up the bank and ran to get under the showery waterfall. Water was cold on our backs and made us squirm and squeal. I let it run on my hair, too, which was cut in a short, straight bob for the summer. It felt good to turn my head back and let the water splash right on my face like a gentle rain.

Suzanne and I rubbed each other's backs with a bar of soap kept handy on a little stone ledge under the overhang of the brook's bank. She was five and still had a babyish roundness to her face, but her hair had darkened, was hardly blond at all anymore. We had kind of hoped she was going to stay blonde and look like Mamma's childhood pictures. Not a one of us was blonde.

Suzanne got a lot of special treatment being the baby. At least I thought so. When we raced and I won, it was no big thing. An eight-year-old was supposed to win. But when Suzanne won, she earned cheers and applause. But there were advantages to being older, all the same. For instance, I could climb much higher in any tree.

The falls was formed by a deep drop-off in little Ramble Brook. There was never a lot of water going over, but it was a nice stream with enough room for a grown man to stand under it. The boys were still splashing each other as Suzanne and I ran to the pine thicket where we'd hung our outer clothes on a limb.

Pulling a dress down over wet, cold skin was uncomfortable. It wouldn't slide very well and wanted to stick under my arms. Then when I finally got it down, it clung to my very wet underpants. I was helping Suzanne with her dress when I heard Daddy's whistle calling us home. I was almost sure it was the second time he'd blown it. I could tell because of the sound of impatience in it. I crumpled my hands into a fist-whistle and quickly answered. When Daddy called, we came, no matter where we were or what we were doing.

The boys had heard it, too, and were scrambling up the bank racing to their clothes and pulling them on as they ran. We ran past Far Field (the farthest field from the house), crawled between horizontal hickory poles forming a gate called Apple Bars, and walked on past crab apple trees lining a rough tractor road. From there we ran down by the big oak tree with the boys' gabled treehouse peering through its leaves, on across Sand Flat, and finally up Sunny Lawn.

Jackie, our sister four years older than Stanley, who, by the way, still would join our youthful pranks as often as possible, now waited for us at the pasture wall. "Oh, *dear!*" she exclaimed when she saw us up close. "What will we do? You can't see company like that. What in the *world*...?"

"We've been sliding!" said Suzanne gleefully, pulling up her dress to show off her wet pants.

"Who's the company?" Stan asked.

"Oh, their name is Owens. Mrs. Owens bought one of Dad's paintings once, and Mr. Owens was on the jury with him or something like that. They're on their way back to Atlanta now from a trip out west."

"Oh. The curious kind," responded Stan.

"Yes." Jackie lifted her heavy auburn hair to cool her neck.

"Any children?" I asked hopefully.

"Oh, no. They're retired, I think. And wait until you see how *big* they are!" Jackie said as we started to the house.

We trudged up the last bit of hill to Stone Gables. Charles and Stanley skirted around through hedges to get a look at the visitors' car. We all finally clustered around Jackie who said the only thing for us to do was to climb the wall to the upstairs patio and slip in through an east room window. We'd surely be seen if we entered by the patio door on the balcony. Window entrances were far more fun anyway.

There was a place in a little corner by the garage where a high stump made it possible for long legs to climb up and over the patio wall. The stump was beginning to rot having been there since Daddy built the flint and granite house twenty-five years before. So you had to be careful just how you stepped on the stump, or it would crumble.

Stanley went up first, stepping on the stump, then a window ledge. From there he could reach the drain hole at the bottom of the patio wall. Getting a good hold, he walked up slightly protruding stones and pulled himself over the wall. It wasn't really hard for him with his long legs and much experience in the act.

For Charles it wasn't very hard, either. But when it was my turn, I had to have help at both ends, Jackie pushing from below and Stanley pulling from above. They decided Suzanne was too little and when she started crying Jackie put a hand quickly over her mouth. "Oh, don't cry, company'll hear you," she pleaded.

A little mud came off on the spread when we piled through the window and across the bed, but it would brush off when it dried. Anyway, we girls wouldn't mind sleeping under a little mud. I got some clean clothes from Suzanne's drawer in the chiffonier to throw down to Jackie.

As I dressed I could hear the friendly rumble and murmur of voices down in the Hall. Daddy's voice was strong and dominant over all the rest. His voice matched his personality and physical build perfectly. He was tall and straight, often holding his hands behind his back as he talked. If he were angry, his thick gray moustache twitched and the nostrils of his long nose quivered. Behind his glasses, his eyes could twinkle with approving cheer or gleam in stern reprimand. Sometimes he kept his safari-type helmet on even in the house so you couldn't always see his bald spot and the fringe of gray hair around it. But he really wasn't ashamed of his bald spot. It was just that he was so sensitive to strong light.

In fact, his oversensitivity to the light, along with a very bad eye problem, was the reason for his early retirement as an artist. I had never seen him paint, but often wished I could, partly because I would like to see him creating a beautiful picture, and partly because if he could paint still, maybe he and Mamma wouldn't have time to teach us at home, and we could go to public school. It would be fun to ride the school bus.

After giving my hair a last brushing, I met the boys in the little vestibule outside the two bedrooms. We tiptoed toward the balcony just far enough to look down on the tops of the visitors' heads. They both had gray hair and, as Jackie had said, were very large. That was all I saw before I stepped back quickly. The lady tipped her head back to look up and around curiously. Charles didn't get out of sight quickly enough.

"She saw me," he whispered.

We loved to have company, but we were all as shy as wild deer. We were curious and wanted to see everything and everybody, but we didn't usually want to be seen, unless the visitor was someone we knew very well. There weren't many of those at our house which was set one-half mile from the highway, approached by a rough, rutted road.

"Let's go back down over the roof and come in from the outside," suggested Stanley, letting his whisper rise almost to conversational volume.

Before we could climb across the bed to reach our exit window, Daddy called out to us, "All right, children, come on down. These folks won't bite you!"

We had been discovered. We went slowly across the upper balcony, down a short flight of steps, inched along the lower balcony, and down the long flight. At that point Charles slid down the shiny rail, which he always did, his feet barely touching the bottom step as he leaped to a certain gray-green floor slate.

The Owenses were very affectionate and insisted on hugging us all and kissing some of us. Charles and Stan managed to duck out of their kisses. Suzanne, prodded by Jackie, arrived from the back with a corner of her dress hem in her mouth. She and I didn't get away from the kisses. The Owenses sat back down, their rocking chairs creaking and groaning. Suzanne and I sat on the window seat, comforted by the distance between us and the strangers.

They stayed for supper. Mamma called us out one at a time to come help her, and for once we weren't sorry. We left in very polite silence, but the minute we were out of sight around the breakfast room archway, we burst into giggles. Charles and Stanley were sent to kill a rooster before they milked the cow. Daddy usually killed the roosters or hens, but someone had to keep the Owenses entertained so they wouldn't wander back into the kitchen. Mamma didn't want Daddy's Atlanta friends to see the dark cobwebby corners or the wood-smoked ceiling.

Suzanne and I were put to work shucking and silking corn out on the big stone under the north dogwood. Sunshine was only touching the very top of the dogwood this late in the afternoon. The dogs, Thor and Crusoe, sat in a semicircle around us eyeing us expectantly, their tongues dripping. "It's only corn, Crusoe," said Suzanne conversationally. "You know you don't want raw corn."

About then the chickens raised an uproar at the chopping of the rooster's head. Thor and Crusoe started barking and running about, and Charles came tearing around the corner of the garage looking white and holding his hand over his mouth. Stanley had to finish the job alone.

After supper that night, the big girls sang over the dishpan in their usual gaiety. Ginger was home for the summer, so Jackie had someone just older than herself to pal around with. We loved having Ginger home from Rabun Gap School. Her long wavy dark hair framed a slender face lit up by sparkly brown eyes. She brought us crazy songs to learn like "John Jacob Jingle Hyman Smith" and she could always think of something fun to do.

Mamma came in from the Hall looking anxious. She reached up to replace a hairpin in the neat brown bun at the back of her head. "The Owenses are going to spend the night, girls, so I want you to prepare the east room for them when you finish the dishes. Be sure and use the nice sheets, not those I made."

"But, Mamma," said Jackie as she dried a handful of silverware, "what—what if they break the bed down?"

"Oh, Jackie, they won't break it down!" said Ginger.

"I'm not real sure," said Mamma as she wiped crumbs off the bin cover and dusted them into the trash. "But we have to give them a bed."

I followed Mamma back into the Hall and pulled a little stool up next to her chair. It was only when we had company that we even sat in the Hall. In winter we sat in Daddy's study-bedroom for evening reading, but in summer by the time we came in from playing the dusk into dark, it was time for bed. I drank in the beauty of the tall carved walnut bookcases, their glass doors reflecting a kerosene lamp which sat on a marble-topped stand. The lamplight glinted softly on highly polished gray and green slates and was reflected in the tall west windows which needed no curtains since there was a heavy canopy of ivy outside.

We listened to the tales the Owenses told, at first with much interest, then as they were repeated, with slightly less enthusiasm. By the time they launched into the third telling of how they got lost in Chicago, Daddy was fidgeting noticeably in his chair.

When there was a slight pause between stories, Daddy rose quickly and said cheerfully, but authoritatively, "We will have our evening verses now. Won't you join us?" The Owenses heaved themselves up from their chairs and filled in the vacancy we left for them in our circle.

This was such a natural daily occurrence to us that we never thought how terrifying it might be to someone who hadn't memorized lots of Bible verses. We were constantly learning new ones so we wouldn't say the same ones every night. What was really crushing was to be ready to say "Jesus wept" and have the one next to you say it ahead of you. Then you had to think quickly of another one.

Mr. Owens was standing beside me, and I could hear him breathing harder and harder as each one around the circle said a verse. It came closer and closer to his turn. I was really embarrassed for him when he choked and stammered, finally saying, "Now I lay me down to sleep...oh, that's not from the Bible. Go on, little girl."

After the last one had said a verse, we knelt on the hard, cool slate floor. It was automatic to us. But it was not for the Owenses. Daddy waited politely until with much huffing and puffing they had eased themselves down. Then he started the Lord's Prayer, and we all said it together. There was something about this time every evening with the cool slates under me, the warmth of brothers and sisters around me, and the deep tones of Daddy's voice leading our prayers that made me feel very secure and at peace. But I think the Owenses were glad when it was all over.

However, they snapped back in fine form. As Daddy helped Mrs. Owens to her feet, he was saying firmly but courteously, "And now Eula will show you to your room. We rise early here." But Mr. Owens was already beginning another tale as he fell back into his groaning chair. Daddy looked disgusted, but they didn't notice.

After a few more minutes of polite listening, almost beyond his endurance, Daddy cleared his throat loudly and said, "Well, all good things must come to an end. Hope you two sleep well..."

"You know, the best part of the trip...," began Mr. Owens.

Mamma said to Mrs. Owens, "I'll just check and be sure the girls got everything ready for you. Would you like to come with me?"

"Oh, no, thank you, I'll just sit right here. This is so restful, you know. I could just sit here all night, I believe."

The Seth Thomas clock on the mantle at the other end of the Hall struck eleven o'clock cheerfully and loudly. "Well, the old clock seems to be saying good night," remarked Daddy starting to rise.

"Dear, do tell them about getting arrested for speeding and how they almost put you in jail," said Mrs. Owens rocking placidly.

My eyes were getting very heavy since it was way past my bedtime, but I didn't want to give up and actually go to bed before I was told. Suddenly I realized all the others except Suzanne and me had gone out. I went to see what was going on and Suzanne followed right behind.

"Do it, Ginger, please do it," Jackie was pleading as I opened the double doors into the kitchen.

"Somebody's got to do something," said Stanley. "I think I'll

throw up if that woman mentions one more time how big the Wrigley sign is in Chicago."

"Okay. But you will have to help me think of the right songs," said Ginger.

We followed her out the corridor, through the garage, and into the moonlit night. We stationed ourselves near one of the big hemlocks, and Stanley held a hymnbook while Jackie held the flashlight. Ginger lifted her precious silvery cornet to her lips and started playing. The clear notes echoed from dark shadows of Tulip Hill and filled all the quiet, gone-to-sleep corners with sound. But it was the titles of the songs Ginger played that were to urge (we hoped) our visitors to bed: "Why Do You Wait, Dear Brother?," "Day Is Dying in the West," "Almost Persuaded," and finally "The Morning Light is Breaking."

We swished our feet in the dew-wet grass as we started back in, giggling and jostling each other. It may have had nothing to do with the concert, but the Owenses were climbing the stairs when we appeared. Ginger put her cornet in its case and said guiltily, "I really shouldn't have done that." But neither Mamma nor Daddy scolded her for it. In fact, I thought I heard Daddy already snoring.

I went to bed with Suzanne on a pallet in the west room. Ginger and Jackie had one double bed, Stanley and Charles the other.

After Ginger blew our light out, I closed my eyes and listened to the rise and fall of insect songs through the open windows. I went to sleep so quickly with the sun-scented sheet pulled up close to my chin that I never would have known if the Owenses *had* broken our bed down. But it was still whole the next day.

As shy as we were of company, we sang out with the greatest of glee, "Somebody's coming!" when we saw the flash of sunlight on a windshield as a rare car crept up our rough road. We'd spy on guests from a thick abelia hedge to see if there were cousins to play with or if it were long-faced grown-ups from whom we'd stay hidden and would hope not to be called.

Rev. and Mrs. Ray Johnson and their family were favorite company for me because their daughter Ruthie was only a little younger than I. I dearly loved to play with her. Also, Mamma got out the heirloom silver when they came to dinner, delicate pieces with names of Grandmother's family engraved on the handles. Charles said those silly forks didn't make big enough bites and he was glad there weren't enough to go around so he could use the every day ones. I always hoped I could use Grandmother Grace's spoon.

Reverend Johnson, pastor of Clarkesville Baptist Church for several years, sometimes came by himself just to talk to Daddy. They'd talk for hours on deep subjects, quote a lot of scripture to each other, and poetry, too. Sometimes we'd be surprised in church when Rev. Johnson would refer in his sermon to something our father had said. Always before Rev. Johnson left our house Daddy would call us from all corners of the place to have prayer with him. Rev. Johnson was a really good prayer. He would pray for an awfully long time so your knees went numb and your eyes got so tired of being squeezed shut you started parading stories across the backs of your lids.

One time as Rev. Johnson was praying there came a loud knock at the door. I opened one eye cautiously to see what Daddy was going to do. He didn't do anything. Rev. Johnson kept praying. That doorknocker was so loud it was very hard to keep yourself planted and not leap right out of your skin. But there was no doubt in our minds, if Rev. Johnson was still praying, and Daddy still kneeling, then we'd better keep quiet, too. On the third big bamming knock, Rev. Johnson drew his prayer to a quick end. Daddy rose in one fluid motion and strode to the door.

Mamma tried to make polite conversation with Rev. Johnson, but Daddy's encounter at the door had our attention.

"Mr. Knight, I've come to talk to you about the tractor you were interested in."

"What tractor was that?" Daddy asked calmly.

About then Charles was slipping behind Mamma and easing toward the breakfast room arch.

"That's the John Deere, sir, model # _____. I have your reply card here in my satchel. You are Charles C. Knight, aren't you?"

Daddy laughed. "Let me call him for you. You have the wrong Mr. Knight. Charles! Charlie Boy, come here. This gentleman wants to speak to you."

Charles was almost gone, only one brown heel still showing around the corner as he disappeared into the kitchen. But his ears were working fine and he had to come back. When that tractor salesman saw that Charles C. Knight was maybe ten or eleven years old, he didn't have much more to say, but Daddy

did have a few things to say to Charles about answering adver-
tisements for free inquiries. And Rev. Johnson had a huge laugh
out of it. Charles's ears turned very pink. That episode didn't
stop him from answering ads, but did make him a bit more cautious, I think.

How we loved it when Aunt Emma and Uncle Pete brought us
cousins with whom to play. Or when Porter Harris, fiddler like
no other, brought his four children who were so much fun:
David, Phyllis, Johnny, and little Mark. Or when the Alleys
came, or the Kinneys from right up the road. Or the Gardners
from Jacksonville who came to rent the cottage for many wonderful summers. Or Mr. and Mrs. Starr Peck from Atlanta.

Mr. Peck could find quarters in our ears, lose a half dollar up
toward the rafters somewhere, then call it back, a shining disc on
the back of his wrist. Julia Peck, his wife, would sit straight as
Queen Victoria, hands crossed on her knees and a tiny smile
lighting her eyes while we watched the coin tricks. Our timidity
gave way to curiosity and utter awe as we edged closer and
closer to the swift-handed magician.

When Mamma's cousin and his wife came from Commerce in
their farm truck our shouts of "Somebody's coming!" were even
more jubilant and we certainly didn't stay hidden in the abelia
row. We called those wonderful folks Uncle Henry and Aunt
Joyce and there was never a doubt they loved children. Uncle
Henry patiently waited for all of us to scramble up in his truck
for a ride the last few hundred feet to the house. And when they
left he'd smile fondly while we all piled up again, older ones
helping the younger ones. One time they pleaded with Mamma
and Daddy to let Ginger and Jackie go home with them to play
with their daughters Miriam and Barbara. I was terribly envious
when the rest of us had to clamber down from that truck out at
the highway and let the girls ride on with the wind blowing their
hair out behind them like feathery kites.

The occasion of having company at Stone Gables held its haz-
ards. There might be unwanted hugs or even kisses. You might
have to climb over the roof to get to your clean clothes and stay
up half the night. But there was great entertainment with poetry
recitals, song fests, traveler's stories, riddles, and magic tricks.
From the time the lucky Number One Spy first sang out, "Somebody's coming!" until the tail lights bumped down the hill, a
certain energy charged the very atmosphere like the feeling of
anticipation when Cousin Flora's annual big box of surprises

arrived from Pennsylvania. You just never knew what interesting things might happen, such as a cat having kittens in the middle of the Hall floor while the preacher and his wife tried to ignore Mamma's attempts to make her stay out.

Things went kind of flat when weeklong guests were all gone. But Mamma hummed happily as she hung sheets on the line.

Chapter Three
The Season of...
Spring

Many events that took place at Stone Gables and Pinedale are intertwined with the changing of seasons in my memory. As spring splashes joy across the landscape, I remember the feel of freshly hoed dirt under my feet in Mamma's garden, and Mamma's big straw hat, and the way she hummed under her breath as she worked. As summer comes on with a slow hum of bees, other things come to mind like catching fireflies, rolling in itchy grass, or eating lunch perched in a tree. And so the memories play into autumn and then winter. It's really hard to say which might be my favorite season, but spring seems like the one that starts everything.

When jonquils began to put green points up through February's cold ground, Daddy would often remark something about "God's annual resurrection picture." When tiny pink leaves appeared on maple trees and frogs opened their chorus in our pond, it was time for the house wren to return to her nest under the garage eave.

The first really clear memory that stayed with me as a child was of something that happened in the spring. It was an event of such magnitude that I would have remembered it no matter when it happened. But it did happen in the spring of 1946.

Finally it was warm enough for us to go barefoot. All day we had played in the grass and walked tender-footed across pebbled places. It was such fun that I didn't even know Mamma had gone to bed sick. But, as any three-year-old would, I missed her when it started getting dark and when it was suppertime.

"Mamma's sick in her room and Dr. Garrison's here," said

37

Ginger in answer to my inquiry. Seeing my eyes get very big, Jackie said, "She's not bad sick. It's sort of a special sickness. She'll be okay."

"Will she kiss me good night?" I wanted to know.

"No, silly," said Charles. He really wasn't so very big, only six. He didn't know what was going on either. Nor did he understand how a sickness could be "special."

We went out after supper and inspected the doctor's car. Stanley and Charles estimated how fast the car would run. I stood on the running board and peered in at the gray upholstery. Ginger came out and said it was bedtime.

"We'll just wash our feet one time in the nice wet grass," said Stanley. He was very gook at stalling.

The dew had fallen heavily. We swished through the grass until our feet were squeaky clean. Then we tiptoed into the house. Ginger said to be very quiet. All you could hear as we went up to bed were the stairs creaking here and there.

Daddy came to tuck us in. He asked if we'd enjoyed our supper. Then he said there would be a surprise for us tomorrow. But by now all I wanted was Mamma's good night kiss and the little pat she always gave me on the cheek. Daddy's beard was rough, and he didn't know how to fix the covers right. Squirming down under the quilt, I sobbed, and Daddy patted me helplessly on the back, but it didn't make me feel better. Finally he told me I could go back downstairs with the big girls.

It was five minutes after midnight, according to Daddy, when a funny squeaky cry came from Mamma's room. Daddy soon came out smiling. I said, "Could I see Mamma now, please."

After a quick consultation with the doctor, Daddy ushered me in. Mamma smiled at me and my world was all right again. I looked at the tiny red baby they showed me and wondered what you were supposed to do with something like that. Daddy said it was a sister, but I thought sisters were supposed to be big enough to fix supper.

Anyway, it was fine because Mamma smiled at me, and Daddy patted my head. Dr. Garrison said I was such a big girl he'd just have to give me a dollar bill, and he did. It was a funny feeling piece of paper. Charles tried to talk me out of it the next day by offering me his rusty dump truck. But I didn't trade.

That was the beginning of spring in April—a barefoot-full-of-flowers-and-fun spring. And it was the beginning of my new sister, Suzanne.

But spring was not just a time of birth. The next spring after Suzanne was born death touched our family.

It was almost night, yet for some reason Daddy was putting water in the radiator of the car, getting ready to go somewhere. Mamma was packing her bag. It had something to do with that man in a taxicab who had just come and gone.

I hung around while Mamma packed, hoping to go, too. She had her lips pressed close together, and she wasn't humming a song at all. Anyone who was getting ready to go somewhere would be happy, I thought. But something was wrong this time.

"Where are you going?" I asked. "I want to go."

"I'm going to Grandma's," she said and bit her lip. "You can't go this time, Honey. You see, Grandma can't see you now. She's gone—she's gone to live with Jesus."

There were tears in Mamma's eyes, and I felt tears in mine, too. But mine were for Mamma, not for Grandma.

I tried to remember how Grandma looked. But all I could picture was a very big bed with a lady in it to whom I was handed to be kissed. I couldn't remember her face even though she had kissed me so many times. But she was soft, I remembered, soft and warm.

It was not hard to remember going to Aunt Emma's house. That's where Grandma had lived since Grandfather died and she broke her leg. I loved Aunt Emma's biscuits right from the warming closet without any jelly, and I liked to look at the hogs rooting in their pen. My cousin Phyllis had a wonderful playhouse with all kinds of dishes under a privet hedge. There was a big pecan tree in the yard, too, and we could eat all the nuts we could find in the fall. Also, there was a swing on the porch like the one at our cottage, only bigger and faster.

Mamma picked Baby Suzanne up and nuzzled her neck. Then she said to me, "You help your big sisters take care of the baby. Help keep her from doing things that will hurt her; she's so little! Mamma will be gone a few days, and Daddy will be gone some, too. You be a sweet girl, will you?"

All I could do was nod and then hide my face in her coat. Then Daddy came to carry her bag down, and they got in the car which was already cranked up and roaring at the front door. Mamma waved to us and even smiled a little.

It was a dreary evening. Suzanne cried a lot. Everyone looked as if they were just about to cry, especially Ginger and Jackie. When Ginger put me to bed I said, "What is it like to go and live with Jesus? Is it terribly bad?"

"Why, no, it's—it's wonderful to live with Jesus, Brenda. It's like—well, it's like getting to sit on Mamma's knees all the time, or whatever you like the most to do."

"Grandma wouldn't care to sit on Mamma's knee. She's too big."

"Well, of course not. But she will be able to talk with Jesus, and he will tell her how much he loves her. And she will have all the flowers she wants without having to wait for someone to bring them to her. Maybe she'll be able to dig again," she added thoughtfully.

"Do they have big beds in heaven? Grandma will have to have one of those that rolls up so she can sit up to kiss the children."

Ginger swallowed and started to cry, and I wondered what I had said wrong.

"But, see," she finally said, "Grandma will be able to walk again in heaven. Jesus may even take her hand himself to show her how."

"Well, then, why are you crying?" I asked.

"Because—just because I'll miss her so much," she said, and she buried her head in the pillow beside me. One of her long braids, curled at the end, fell over in my face.

I looked out the window at stars so bright in the sky and wondered where heaven was and why, if it was so wonderful, everybody cried when someone went there.

There were other things to wonder about as my fifth birthday came and went and I became big enough to walk the mile and a half to Sunday School. One thing that was puzzling was how Jesus could be with me when it was dark and I was scared and still be with Grandma, too.

Another thing that was hard to understand was how God could love everybody. That's what Ginger said, and that's what Mamma and my Sunday School teacher said. But—everybody? That would mean even that drunk man who came stumbling through our woods one day. It would mean all those terrible people who'd made a war in the whole world. And it would mean me when I told lies, like that there weren't any eggs in the hens' nests when really I had dropped and broken them all and hidden them behind a tree.

Anyway, it was good to know that someone loved me so much. And I liked Sunday the best of any day in the week. Of

course that was partly because Sunday was one of the days Charles didn't have lessons, and he could play with me.

Getting ready for Sunday took all day Saturday. It was a day of scrubbing, dusting, cooking, and ironing. I didn't like Saturday much because it was the day someone washed my hair. And if Mamma scrubbed us behind the ears on other days, she scraped us behind the ears on Saturday.

Daddy organized a shoe polishing crew on Saturday night and quizzed us all to make sure those who could read had studied their Sunday School lessons. He started polishing a shoe from heel to the toe and said, "Never let me catch you with only your toes polished. If you don't complete the job, let it be your heels that shine the most. I'll have no hypocrites in my house!" (I sure hoped I never turned into one of those things because they sounded really terrible.)

On Sunday morning you'd find everybody trying to get into the right size socks, Mamma knotting the boys' ties, and one of the big girls always fixing my hair while I tried not to cry. It was a shame for something as nice as "going to church" to be preceded by so much pain.

Sometimes we rode in the Packard to Sunday School, but if John or Brantley weren't home to drive us, we walked. My favorite part of the walk was by a beautiful pasture where there were always horses grazing and where a happy brook chattered over smooth stones as it ran under the road. Charles investigated the brook too closely one Sunday and had to spend church time in the park letting his shoes dry! Somehow he didn't look very sad about that.

Neither Mamma nor Daddy were going to church much at that time. Daddy had all but retired from public life when his eyes became so bad he couldn't read anymore and when bright lights began giving him such terrible headaches. He and Mamma listened to the morning sermons on the radio in Daddy's study while Suzanne played around their feet.

Their absence didn't mean a lack of interest in whether we listened at church, though. Daddy always wanted to know what we'd learned and was rather stern if each one of us couldn't formulate some sensible comment. Once I had spent the whole Sunday School hour studying my teacher's face, observing the way her lips moved when she talked and how the lisp she had made little bright shoots of saliva come out on words like "Samson." I wanted to be able to talk just like that. But it didn't seem as important when Daddy asked me about the Bible story and I couldn't remember who Samson was.

Jackie saw me start to turn red and came to my rescue. "Oh, Dad," she said quickly, "the choir was so funny this morning. They sang, 'I'll Fly Away in the Morning,' and it was as if those big old husky men were trying to fly in their little white robes!"

Daddy laughed and called to Mamma in the kitchen, "Our Jackie has quite a sense of humor." Then he impulsively put an arm around her and squeezed her tight. I slipped out the back door quickly, glad to be forgotten for the moment.

Ginger was sitting with me on a nice warm rock above the stable one spring day teaching me a new Bible verse to use that night. It was John 3:16—about how much God loved me. I started wondering again how he could love me so much. I looked up in the sky that was as blue as the dress Pat had sent me for my sixth birthday. Then I looked at the rambling roses on the stable wall just opening in little pink lacy puffs. How could God have time for me when he was tending to all these other things like making baby cows and roses grow?

"Brenda, you're not even trying to learn this," said Ginger. Then she looked at me and asked, "What's bothering you? Is something wrong?"

"No, I don't guess so," I answered, gazing down at the scuffed toes of my brown oxfords.

"Listen, what is it? Maybe I can help."

"Well," I stammered, not really knowing what to say, "I just don't see why God loved me that much. I mean—enough to let Jesus die. I wish he wouldn't have died."

"But he isn't dead now. He's right here with us. And he does care very much whether you're happy or not."

"But why?" I insisted.

Ginger thought for a minute and curled the end of one braid around her finger. "Maybe you don't have to understand why God loves you. The important thing is just to believe that he does."

A robin lit in a sourwood tree nearby, singing a bubbly song. Just below the pasture wall there was the munching of a cow chewing her cud. After a minute I said, "If Jesus loves me so much, what can I do to show I care for him and thank him? What can I give him? He really doesn't need anything."

Ginger's face had a very tender expression as she reached out to brush my bangs out of my eyes. "No, he doesn't need anything, but he wants it. He wants you to love him. He wants to take care of you like a father who is always there. What would really make him happy would be for you to tell him that you love him and you trust him to take care of you for always and always."

"Is that all?"

"That's a lot."

We prayed together. After I said my little prayer, the exact words of which I never could remember, a warmth much sweeter than the sunshine filled me and surrounded me. And there was a feeling of freedom as a butterfly must surely know when it bursts from its cocoon.

Not long afterwards, I attempted to join the church during a Sunday School assembly program. It hadn't occurred to me, as I went down the aisle, that it wasn't the proper time; I just knew what I wanted to do. The poor Sunday School superintendent looked red and sweaty, and his hand felt limp when I insisted on shaking it. Jackie lamented later that I even dropped my home-made pocketbook in the aisle for everyone to see!

Daddy told me kindly that six wasn't old enough to be a church member. But six was old enough to trust Jesus. I knew that.

Spring was births and deaths and new beginnings, and spring was a trip to the mountains...

We seldom went anywhere except to church and to the grocery store. But at least twice a year we went on a mountain trip, usually in the spring and in the fall. In spring the wild azalea, laurel, and rhododendron were a splendid show; in fall the mountains were banks of red, gold, and purple as the leaves changed color. Besides, in spring or fall it was nice sweater weather, and the sun wasn't so bright for Daddy's eyes if he wore his helmet and covered his window with a piece of cardboard. (I wished he wouldn't do that. It made it look to other people as if there weren't glass in the window.)

One morning above the warm weight of a quilt snuggling my ear I heard my name called. "Wake up! Wake up! Don't you want to go to the Smokies?"

Not hearing clearly what the urgent voice was saying and thinking that the person was getting me up to go to the bathroom, I tried to hide deeper under the covers. Then the word came through—the Smokies! I came up, suddenly wide awake.

Ginger dressed Suzanne, and Jackie made her arms into wings reaching behind to button her own dress. In the west room the boys piled out, too, and we knew by his shout as he descended the stairs that Charles was sliding down by banister, probably with shoes in hand instead of on his feet.

"All right, it's your turn," said Jackie to me, giving her hair one last brushing. "I thought you'd never wake up. Don't you want to go?"

I didn't even bother to answer. Who wouldn't want to go to the Smokies even if you did always have to sit in the front seat because you got carsick?

Outside, the moon was still shining brightly. You could see the dark outlines of the gabled garage roof and shadowy tree shapes against the sky. A rooster crowed just about the time Ginger blew the light out and started us down the dark stairs.

We always left early when we went on mountain trips. Daddy liked early morning anyway, was often up at that time himself, out pulling weeds and pruning bushes. He said it was good to get a lot of road behind us before the traffic picked up. And we didn't mind. It was sort of spooky and really adventurous to start out at four a.m. on a trip.

In the kitchen Mamma had poured for each a glass of milk and cut for each a piece of bread. "I don't know about you, though, Brenda," she said. "You better not drink much. Give some of yours to Stan." I knew what she meant and gave it all to him.

Daddy had the Packard cranked up and roaring outside. The cows had been milked and the fire smothered in the kitchen stove. "About ready, Eula?" Daddy called. "It's time we were already on the road."

"Well, here's the lunch. Run on, children. I'm coming. Here, Suzanne, you put this sweater on."

I wiggled into the backseat hoping Suzanne would be put in the front this time. But as Daddy adjusted his helmet he said, "Where's little Brandy Brew? Let her sit right here between John and me."

"Yes, it's the best place for her," said Mamma. "You girls trade places."

John grinned down at me hopefully, "You will keep your knees out of the way of the gear shift, won't you?" I nodded, knowing that it would be as impossible as it is to whisper when you have something terribly important to say.

The dogs barked all the way down the hill and out the lane—

big German Shepherd Thor and little mongrel Crusoe. "Oh, the dogs will miss us," moaned Suzanne watching them wag their tails in near-darkness as we pulled onto the highway turning north.

We were almost to Rabun Gap, about thirty-five miles, when I had to poke John with my free hand, the other one held tightly to my mouth. He pulled over quickly with a disgusted grunt. "Why does she have to get sick every time?" he complained. I heard Mamma answer as she wiped my forehead with a damp cloth, "She's just not a good traveler like you, son. But she'll be all right now."

I so hoped Mamma was right, and that time she was. As much as I wanted to see everything the others pointed out ("Look at that pretty girl," "She's got a dog," "Man, what a car—it's passing us," "Oh, no, on this narrow road?" "Oh, look at the sun coming up!" "The mountains are purple the way the song says they are!"), I went to sleep. I slept slumped against Daddy's leather jacket (with only a faint consciousness of my knees being shifted along with the gear shift) until we were climbing high into the mountains. I woke to hear everyone's voices muffled: "There went mine," "Yes, mine, too," " Have yours popped yet?" And I could tell by the pressure on my own ears what they were talking about.

I peered over the hood and looked out into blue space. Daddy said, "The dear old mountains are still keeping guard." The mountains were all around us. I squinted through the crook of his arm as he shielded his head with his helmet tipped on one side. Far, far below the silver thread of a river tumbled and turned.

As we climbed sharply upward and as John shifted gears again, Mamma exclaimed, "Oh, look here, girls, at the laurel and azalea. They're more beautiful every year."

Wild azalea blazed from either side of the road, steeply up to the left, dizzily down to the right. There were orange, lemon, and pink ones in no planned pattern, some blooming boldly close to the edge of the bank, some shyly hiding behind the trees, barely showing at all. Laurel was shyer in color, a delicate pink, but there were frothy clouds of it all along. If some laurels were slower blooming, the glossy leaves made up for a lack of blossoms as sunlight touched them into a shimmer.

Daddy said he had to have some water to splash on his forehead, so we stopped by a little water slide that made a gentle roaring kind of song trickling down from its dark beginning place on the forested mountainside. Ginger found a clump of purple violets close by and picked one, sticking it in a buttonhole. I tried to take one of the brilliant orange flowers from an overhanging azalea bush, but Daddy scolded me. "What would happen if everyone broke a limb from a bush?" he asked. I hadn't thought about it like that.

The climb on foot up to the top of Clingman's Dome was the end of the trip. After that we would eat and start home, I heard Daddy say. I walked as fast as I could trying to keep up with Stanley and Charles. Beautiful little wild flowers bloomed by the trail, and I could almost imagine a bear coming through the spruces and firs where the shadows intermingled. There were signs that said, "Do Not Feed the Bears," but we never saw any, and Mamma was glad.

At the top I licked my dry lips as I looked over the guard rail at range after range of mountains. "Wouldn't it be wonderful to be a bird," cried Jackie. "Or better still to be human and have wings, too!"

"There's the road we came on. See that curve?" said Stanley pointing. "Hey, Charles, look. There is a waterfall below the road where we thought we heard it roaring. See that splash of white?"

"You know," said John thoughtfully, "the mountains in Japan are supposed to be about the most beautiful in the world, but they're not as pretty as these to me."

"Could be because you were in the army when you saw them."

"Could be. Hey, sports, how about taking a short-cut back to the parking lot? Not you," he said shaking his head at me.

We had our picnic by the roadside back down the mountain a ways where a glistening cold spring came down over black rocks. There were boiled eggs, sandwiches, and homemade cookies—Mamma's own "rock" cookies. I was feeling good then and refused to let Stan talk me out of my roast beef sandwich.

"This cold spring water is delicious. Tastes like ferns," commented Mamma, catching some more in a cup.

"A little quiet spot like this is far better than one of those modern picnic areas with the touch of man everywhere," Daddy said as he walked back and forth in the shade. "'I will lift up mine eyes unto the hills from whence cometh my help...'" he quoted. His voice reminded me of the waterfall we had heard, booming with something to be triumphant about.

It was a beautiful day. The air tasted like the spring water, ferny and cool. You could close your eyes and taste the sky, the spruces, and the mossy rocks.

Packed back into the car, two layers in the back, with Charles in the front this time (much to my delight), we started home. We stopped several times for water or to see a particularly beautiful azalea or to look at the mountains from a wide-open place. As the curves turned back and forth dizzyingly, I hid my face, hoping the wave of hot nausea would go away. Sleep came to my rescue again, and I didn't wake until sundown when we were driving into Clayton, only thirty miles from home.

As we pulled up to a traffic light, Daddy said, "Look for a place to stop for ice cream, son." My hand tightened on the holding strap, and Suzanne and I grinned at each other. It was almost too wonderful to stand. I licked my cone so slowly, trying to make it last as long as it would, that Ginger threatened to eat it for me. It dripped down the front of my dress.

The dogs met us at the entrance to Pinedale, wagging their tails and barking with joy. "Oh, I wish you could have gone, too, Crusoe," Suzanne called out the window.

"Heaven forbid," said John under his breath, and Daddy laughed.

The sound of the wheels running through wet sand echoed from the trees shouldering close to the lane. As we rounded the south bend at the top of the hill, I could see the dear dark outline of Stone Gables and the great tall elm towering above it. The car lights glinted on the windows and then we were home again. The sweet smell of spring was everywhere. Suzanne was hugging Crusoe and letting him lick her face, and the boys had Thor almost climbing on them. I ached because I wanted to hug everything, but there seemed no way.

Part of spring was helping plant the garden and the smell of tomato plants, fresh earth, and stable fertilizer. Spring was picking wild strawberries and having strawberry shortcake. It was finding a vireo's nest hanging from a low limb, and it was driving the cow back to pasture with a stomach full of goodies from Mamma's flower beds. Spring was when you felt like a locust that's just come out of its skin. You hoped your skin would never get tough again and that you could always feel every feathery breeze and shaft of sunlight.

Spring was the smell of wild onions in the air and the taste of them in the milk. Mamma would give us each a little piece of raw onion to eat before we drank our milk. "Then you won't taste it in the milk," she said. And it really worked. But Charles thought it was crazy. He just didn't drink milk during the wild onion season.

Part of spring, too, was flocks of tiny new biddies following behind clucking, fussing hens. It was the taste of fresh yellow butter on warm homemade bread and buttermilk right from the big brown churn. It was the Laurel House (so called because the thicket of laurel was truly like a house inside) in full bloom; it was red japonica, white bride-like spirea, and the forsythia bushes as yellow as butter. It was soft, fuzzy pink and white balls on oak trees, and it was blooms from tulip poplars fallen in the brook and floating downstream like funny little boats.

And spring brought rains, big rains. You'd wake to hear it on the roof, running off the eaves in streams, and you'd hunch down under the covers as if you thought that next it would be running down your neck. There was one big rain that lasted almost forever.

It rained constantly for two weeks, and on the fourteenth day it was still beating with steady rhythm on the roof. From the east room windows I could glimpse bedraggled chickens lined up under the protective branches of a hemlock tree. The sky looked like old, damp camp-out blankets someone had forgotten to fold up. The crab apple tree that had bloomed like a pink cloud was now its old black, rugged self again except for some tiny green leaves on its thorny branches. Even the pink carpet underneath was all slush now.

Downstairs there were the bass tones of Daddy's voice dictating a letter to Mamma. I crept over to the Little Room to listen, thinking maybe I'd hear something more interesting than my list of ten spelling words I was trying to learn.

"All through the night," Daddy was saying, "the storm that had lines down and transportation locked in other places sang through the pines here like great organ tones—at times it seemed there were voices singing. There were high soprano notes—not too high—and the distant basses made a background."

There was a pause, and I could hear Mamma's pen as she wrote. Then Daddy changed to his conversational voice as he said, "Eula, why has God afflicted me so that I can't see to paint anymore? Look out the window here at the myriad tiny branches in the elm tree etched against the sky. And the background of rain-washed green in varying shades."

"Maybe you could do just a little painting each day," said Mamma quietly, so quietly I could barely hear her.

"You know I cannot!" Daddy snapped unkindly. "I can't even see to read the children's essays. They have to read them to me."

How well I knew that. And how much easier it would be sometimes just to give him an essay and run into the next room or at least pretend to read a book. But to have to read it out loud!

"But," continued Mamma gently, "painting's not the same as reading. Don't you remember how—sometimes—you'd paint just a minute at a time and then come back to it later...?"

"I tell you, I just can't see well enough," said Daddy crossly. My stomach knotted in apprehension at the bitterness of his tone.

"Maybe one of the children could help you on the tedious, close foundation work. You know, Charles is really interested in art."

"Yes, yes, he is, and he's good, too," Daddy agreed in a thoughtful voice. I heard him cross the floor, pick up the iron poker and stir the fire. "Oh, well, I'm thankful that at least I can see the beauty even if I can't reproduce it on canvas. God help me if I ever go completely, helplessly blind! I'd rather be six feet under in a kind pine box. But, Eula, there's the money, too. I don't know how long we're going to hold out on Cousin Flora's legacy check. And we sold the last lot in Florida last year."

"Aren't you going to cut timber again in the fall?"

"Yes. Tarnation! I'm glad I invested in the trees, but I do hate to cut them!"

The poker slammed against the wall. He walked quickly back and forth in the small room. I pictured Mamma having to draw her legs under the straw-bottomed rocker to get out of his way. Then a chair creaked as he sat back down. "Maybe you're right. Maybe I could try to paint a little. Let's get back to this letter to Orman..."

Just then I heard Jackie coming calling my name. I got up as quickly and quietly as I could and appeared around the corner of the bureau as if (I hoped) I had just been looking out the window.

"Brenda, are you ready for me to ask you your spelling words? Mamma said for me to do it this time. What were you doing, eavesdropping again? Sometime you're going to hear something you won't want to hear."

"Well, I didn't this time. They were talking about maybe Daddy's going to paint again."

"That's a terrible sentence. But really? I wish he could!" she said wistfully. "Anyway, on with the lesson. I have some studying of my own to do."

"Don't you wish you could have watched him painting that brown picture of a thick woods in snow?"

"Yes, I do. Or the one of the giant red oak. That's one of my favorites. But now. Spell *write*, that's the kind of write you do on paper."

About dinner time (noon) the rain slowed to a soft patter, and the birds started a chorus from tree to tree. Mamma said that it would clear up soon now, for sure. Stanley went for the mail and came back drenched to the bone. He had had to swim across the bridge over the brook, and he said the river was out of its banks also. Mamma shook her head and looked worried as she and Jackie served plates of beans and meat loaf.

After dinner we played hide-and-seek which left the beds stripped, the dust stirred under the beds, and the closets rearranged. We really tore things up looking for Charles once. He had hidden in the enormous porcelain tub built into the still incomplete bathroom. After that we played records, Stanley and Charles taking turns winding up the Victrola. As long as we played things like "Londonderry Aire," Schubert's "Serenade," or "March of the Wooden Soldiers," everything was fine. But then Suzanne and I chose the chorus of the Indian children which was just a rhythmic chant with drums in the background. It was fun to clap and dance to until the third or fourth time we played it.

Suddenly, then, Daddy's voice boomed like a clap of thunder, "Cut that thing off! If I hear that record one more time, I'm going to break it into pieces!"

Charles was closest to the phonograph and jumped to cut it off. For a minute there was a shaky unnatural silence in which nothing could be heard but the rain. Then Daddy said from right below the balcony, "Charles, you come down. I want to discuss something with you. Stanley, you find something quiet for the little girls to do."

It was late that afternoon when the rain very quietly stopped, and there was only a slow drip off the eaves. To everyone's delight, we ran downstairs, up the corridor, and out the back door.

Suzanne and I tasted the raindrops off sourwood leaves and

ran around in the woods counting mushrooms. Then we discovered something we wondered why we hadn't seen before—there was a rainbow in the sky! With red and orange and pale blue and green all blending together, the bow stretched from the tops of the trees way over in the south woods all the way across the pasture's sky and down to the tops of the trees again. I remembered what Daddy had said about wanting to paint again, and I wished he could paint that rainbow.

We raced towards the house to see who could tell first about the rainbow. But at the door we almost bumped into the boys who had raced from the other direction. They pushed ahead breathlessly and tramped wetly right to the study door. It was Stanley who got his breath first.

"Dam's busted," he gasped.

Daddy's face turned as gray as the rim of hair around his bald spot as he picked up his helmet. But he took an edge off the shock by chiding Stanley briskly for saying "Dam's *busted.*" "No need to use poor grammar," he was saying as the door closed behind them. The back door slammed behind Jackie.

"Can we go, too, Mamma?" I asked.

"Yes, I'll go with you. I don't want you girls getting too close."

"See the rainbow!" exclaimed Suzanne as we walked down the hill. "It was prettier a minute ago. It went all across the sky. Now it's sort of floated apart."

"It's still pretty, though," said Mamma. "And look at the sunlight on pine tree trunks. Oh, if only it hadn't burst!"

The rushing white water tearing through a huge gaping hole in the clay dam was deafening as we walked as close as Mamma would let us. She let us get one good look and then pulled us far back. We couldn't hear what Daddy was saying, but he was motioning and pointing with his hands, already making plans for rebuilding the spillway and filling in the tunneled hole.

"Mamma, will we have the pond again?"

"Why, yes, of course."

"Will the ram still work?" (The ram was a type of pump placed below the dam. It required a powerful flow of water to raise a supply to the house.)

"No, not while the dam's out."

"Well, what will we do?"

"We'll have to carry all our water from the spring."

And so we did. No one ever went down the hill without an empty bucket. And no one climbed back up the quarter-mile trail without a full bucket of sparkling spring water. Even Suzanne had a lard bucket "just her size" to carry.

We didn't carry water for people only. There were special shrubs like the Rhododendron catawbiense which had been regularly watered. As the ground began to get dry again, Daddy said we had to keep all the shrubs watered. "Don't just pour it quickly around the stems," he'd say, knowing that was what we wanted to do. "Let the water drizzle slowly down so the soil will have time to soak it up."

After weeks of painful watering, I began to have a special feeling toward "my" shrubs. I was elated when I noticed new leaves coming out and felt personally involved in how tall this little holly or that juniper became.

We all had a part in building the dam back. The boys (and Daddy early in the morning or after sundown) dug red clay out of the side of the ridge beyond the damsite and carried it by wheelbarrow loads to the hole where, with our bare feet, we packed it and packed it, and the boys tamped it down with ends of two-by-fours. At first the mud would be lumpy, but we'd dampen it and pack it until it was like red concrete.

It was fascinating to see the crazy formations of cracks in the drying mud where the pond had been, and to be able to walk where we could only swim before. But as the summer and swimming weather came, we wished the dam were finished. The merry brook was the only thing pretty about the stumpy pond place. I tried to imagine a nice wide body of water covering ugly mud, and imagine our sticky feet kicking free in a cool lake. It was hard to picture with heatwaves dancing.

Our feet were more tired than they had ever been before, and all but our Sunday clothes stained with red clay before the dam was finished. In the process, we learned that a turtle is extremely hard to kill, that snakes love to sun on warm stones, and that mud has a peculiar smell all its own. We had sung songs at the top of our lungs, silly songs like "There is a boarding house far, far away, where they have ham and eggs three times a day. Oh, how them boarders yell when they hear that dinner bell, Oh, how them eggs do smell three times a day." I think we liked that one particularly because we could practice atrocious grammar! We didn't eat ham and eggs ourselves. Most of the time for lunch it was peanut butter sandwiches delivered to us by Jackie. We must have eaten a gallon of peanut butter building that dam.

One day during the time when water was filling in behind the

repaired dam (oh, wonderful time for tag alders, bull frogs, lily pads, and us), I found Daddy standing in the open west door, hands behind his back, dictating a letter to Mamma who was sitting on the steps. Mamma signaled me to be quiet, and I dropped to the step to listen.

"From the terrace," he dictated, "we look down on the little lake...where a hundred-piece frog orchestra nightly executes antiphonal harmonies joyously. On the other side (on the ridge) the tall tulip trees, rag-barked birches, and stern dark pines look at their reflections in the pool...You will be glad to know that the beautiful water lilies survived the draining of the pond. I watered them each morning, but they are glad now to be able to float their round green rafts again." A mental picture came to me of Daddy coming in all sweaty on so many mornings when most of us were just getting up.

I slipped away to climb a tree and think on the things I had seen and heard. The pond was a pond again; we could go swimming; there would be water on the hill again for people and trees. Everyone was happy. One thing to be very happy about was the fact that summer was finally here, and there were no more lessons. The dogwood tree I was in had a rough and friendly feel as I swung down and did a "skin-the-cat," flipping myself over a limb.

Chapter Four

The Season Of...
Summer

In summertime it got so hot that you could see little heatwaves dancing on Sunny Lawn, and you tried to run around all the stones between the pasture wall and the house because they were hot under your bare feet. Running made a delightful wind on your face, but when you stopped because of a dry mouth and a burning chest, the air smothered close again, hot and still. Walking into the house was like entering a cool, dark cave. For a minute you couldn't see, but you'd walk down the corridor knowing the way without seeing and glorying in the coolness of the concrete walls on either side. Soon your eyes would adjust to sifted light rather than blinding pure sunlight. It felt wonderful to lie tummy-down on the Hall floor until the coolness of the slates had made your face stop steaming.

It was that kind of hot day when I first discovered that Daddy had actually begun painting again. I had been on a long walk hunting pretty stones. After getting a drink of spring water from the cedar bucket in the kitchen, I started upstairs. But something caught my eye. There in the south end of the Hall was an easel. I went to look at the other side of it. A large piece of sandpaper had been tacked to a board; only it wasn't just sandpaper anymore; it had strokes of color on it. Daddy was really painting again, really and truly!

The picture Daddy was painting took form slowly. In minute snatches, he painted. I observed wonderingly how delicately his long fingers held the chalk, the same fingers that worked with rough firewood. It seemed as if his chalk barely touched the paper in floating movements. Though Charles had helped with the

cross-hatching (a blanket of base colors forming a foundation for the picture), Daddy did the rest, tiny bit by tiny bit.

A cabin took form, a stalwart oak close by, other trees in the background, and the white water of a rapids in a stream nearby. The blues and rose and white diffused into a picture that was unrealistic if you looked at it two feet away, but became more true than photography at a distance of fifteen to twenty feet. Photography records facts, Daddy said. An artist's responsibility is to show meaning in the facts.

Daddy couldn't stand for someone to examine one of his pictures closely because they lost their meaning at close range. One visitor was standing right under a painting scrutinizing it when Daddy walked up behind her, cleared his throat peremptorily, and said, "The view was planned for at least fifteen feet away." As he painted he would make a stroke, then step backwards to observe its effect before making another. He had used a mirror to get the distant effect in the twenties and thirties when he painted fulltime in the little shingle-roofed studio.

Daddy was able to make ten or twelve paintings during my young teen years, finding that his eyes, though so weak for any kind of reading, would allow him to paint a little at a time. He was often irritable with us because of the strain of the work, but he was generally much more cheerful than he had been. He was able to do something again; he was truly living again!

Of course this was far different from his earlier life as an artist. Now there was no one knocking at his door asking to buy a painting. There were no exhibits in Atlanta and no rubbing shoulders with other artists who would understand the painful slowness of perfection. No exciting reviews of his art appeared in *The Atlanta Journal* this time. There was only his family to laud him as one painting was finished and a new sheet of paper was tacked to the easel. But we did laud him! It was an exciting time for us.

As each child married, he/she was given a painting as a wedding present. I dreamed of the day when I, too, would reach that great important step and receive a painting, not knowing that Mamma alone would give it to me when the time came. Daddy gave Charles one wonderful picture of a waterfall which Charles himself framed. I was terribly jealous. At fifteen, Charles was certainly not about to get married. But then I hadn't helped Daddy paint, and I couldn't frame a picture, either.

Mamma let Charles and me look at the pictures and sketches

in Daddy's old portfolio one rainy day. Charles studied them. I just looked. That's where we saw the portrait of Mamma, the one that had gotten her and Daddy together in the first place. I thought it was beautiful—that soft golden hair, the face smiling even though the lips were not. But when I asked Daddy why we couldn't put it up somewhere, he said it was a terrible portrait, that he had never been able to capture Mamma's beauty and that, in fact, he had never even tried a portrait after that one. "That picture just isn't good enough to represent your mother," he said.

One late afternoon Daddy came in the west door and called, "There's a beautiful sunset tonight!" Usually I would run to see when he called, but now I barely glanced up from my book. The rule was no reading after sunset until the regular family reading time. I wanted to get every last second of *Little Women* before the sunset was all gone.

I heard Daddy talking to someone down on the front steps and I tried not to listen, not to let his deep voice interrupt the love story of Jo and the professor. But when he said, "I just can't be encouraging at this point, Charlie Boy," my ears pricked up and my eyes left the page. Encouraging in what?

"I've always wished one of you children would become an artist," he said, "but at the same time it's such a hard profession with so little monetary reward unless you're in the right place at the right time. I must just say it would depend on how much you wanted to be an artist. If you wanted to badly enough, you would have to do it; you would have no choice."

I didn't know that Orman, then in Chicago, had reported no sales after months of trying to sell Daddy's paintings. If I had, I would have understood better the wistfulness covered with roughness in Daddy's voice.

By straining against the upstairs window, I could just see Daddy and Charles standing on the steps side by side watching the red colors fade into pink in the sky behind the white pines. Daddy reached over and put his hand on Charles's shoulder. "Whether you paint or preach or saw timber, son, I want you to be able to appreciate a sunset like this, to let it soak inside you and put a peace there that only the good Lord can give."

It was too dark now for *Little Women*. Jackie was running up the stairs to light the kerosene lamp on the landing. I looked at the sky still streaked with color and tried quickly to soak up

some peace. There was the smell of burnt match as Jackie lit the lamp.

It was the blackberry season again, and if Mamma was to get a hundred quarts canned as she did last year, we had to pick hard. So far she only had forty-nine beautiful purple-black quarts lined up on the storeroom shelves. So we started out early one day for the blackberry field over by Hill Switch Road. We ducked to keep from touching the low-hanging limbs along the trail which were drenched with dew.

Jackie found some good bushes for Suzanne and me and then tramped on into the inner jungle of blackberry bushes, blazing a trail as she went. Stanley and Charles stationed themselves over in another section, as usual claiming a spot a bit removed from us girls.

For awhile there were only the sounds of bobwhites calling to each other and the metallic thuds of berries hitting bottoms of lard buckets. Then the bottoms were all covered and you couldn't tell whether someone was picking or not—by the sound, that is. The dew was drying fast, and the sunshine beginning to burn through our protective shirt sleeves.

Jackie started singing "I've Been Working on the Railroad," and we helped her on the "Dinah" part. Stanley belted out bars of "She'll Be Comin' Round the Mountain" and we had great fun adding in all the sound effects. Then he tried one of his tearjerkers, a self-arranged rendition of "My Old Kentucky Home." He knew he could always make me cry with that story/song.

The sun was getting hotter and hotter, and the briar scratches on our hands stung. Suzanne and I looked at our inch or two of berries in despair. A butterfly lit on a bright orange flower not far away. The flower nodded gracefully near to a nice seatlike stone in the edge of the shade.

"I'm not going to quit," I said, trying the big-girl attitude. "I'm going to find a better bush."

"I'm not tired, either," said Suzanne, not to be outdone.

In the distance we heard the roar of an approaching car. The boys made a wild dash to the dirt road about 150 feet away to watch the car from the bushes. You could taste dust after the car had passed. I noticed the boys were pretty slow getting back to their buckets. It sounded as if they were arguing about whether the car was a 1947 or a 1948.

"I'm thinking of someone's initials," called out Jackie. "W. C.

Guess who!"

"Man, woman, or child?" asked Stan from his bush.

"Man."

"Living or dead?" called Charles.

"Living."

"Famous or infamous?" joked Stan.

"Famous!"

"Oh, I know who you mean," Stan said, attacking a low limb heavy with berries. "Winston Churchill. Of course!"

"What took you so long?"

"Just trying to make the game more fun, that's all. Try this one. C. C."

"I know who that is!" I called right back. "That's Carrie Christopher, your girl friend!"

"Okay, smarty!" he affirmed.

Then I tried "D. N." They had a hard time guessing, and Charles scoffed when he found it was Daniel Newsome. That was Pat's latest college beau, and I thought he was nice even if no one else, especially Daddy, seemed to think so.

It seemed as if the insects were getting louder and louder with their raspy song. I suggested to Suzanne that we might sit down on that nice stone for just a few minutes. It was so hot and itchy. We were sitting in the shade trying out some of our blackberries when we heard a twig break in the thicket behind us. It was Stanley and Charles. They put silencing fingers to their lips, so we didn't say anything. We just watched as they slipped along to the garden trail.

"They're going to get cucumbers, I bet," Suzanne said.

"Yeah, you want one?"

"No, I like blackberries better."

After awhile I got to feeling guilty when Jackie started singing "Flow Gently, Sweet Afton" as she steamed out there in the itchy sun. So Suzanne and I found another bush and began to make up for the berries we had obviously eaten.

When the sun was directly overhead we heard the welcome sound of the Tallulah Falls train whistle and knew it was time for dinner. As we came together to compare buckets, I had a sick feeling. There was Jackie with a two-gallon bucket full to the top, and my little bucket was not even half full. Stanley and Charles compared theirs with Jackie's and sort of grinned as if they didn't really care that theirs were way short. Jackie was the one who looked worried.

"Now, what have y'all been doing?" she inquired innocently. "I know you could have gotten more than that. Mamma's going to be disappointed. And Dad won't like it, either; he'll know you've been playing around. He might not even let us go swimming this afternoon."

"Well, too bad," said Stan as he started toward the field gate. "At least I haven't eaten all mine," he said over his shoulder with a grin toward my purple-stained face.

"What did you do anyway?" persisted Jackie, picking a wild daisy and twirling it in her hand as she walked.

"Oh, well, Charles got a briar in his foot, a really bad one. It got down in his shoe somehow. I got it out for him, and then we went to the water hole to cool it. It's doing much better now. He hardly limps, do you, Charlie?"

"No. Oh, no!" said Charles, making a sudden effort to limp just a little bit.

"How in the world..." began Jackie.

"It just got in his shoe somehow, I said."

"But how did it get better so fast? That water must have healing powers. Did it hurt real bad, Charlie?" Jackie asked in commiseration.

Charles stammered. I could tell by the back of his head that whatever he was getting ready to tell was a lie.

"Oh, that's okay," said Jackie. "It was awful hot this morning, and I guess you had to rest awhile."

We walked in silence for a minute. I was wearing some of Charles's old jeans; they made a floppy sound as I walked. When we were almost in sight of the house, Jackie stopped. "Stan," she said, "this bucket's awfully heavy. Why don't you put some of my berries in yours and Charles's buckets?"

Stanley looked dumbfounded. "Now you don't have to do that," he remonstrated, running a hand through his thick hair.

"I know. But it *is* heavy," she insisted.

So they divided the berries and even added a little to Suzanne's and mine. Jackie ended up with no more than Stan had.

As we walked in the back door the shady coolness blessed us. Then the smell of blackberry pie drifted to me, and I knew what we were having for dinner. I would have looked forward to dinner and felt better if I hadn't eaten so many blackberries already and if all the pretty berries in my bucket were ones I had picked myself.

Mamma turned from the hot wood stove and looked at our berries, especially at Stan's and Jackie's. She frowned just a little and wiped a trickle of perspiration off her nose with her apron. Then she said thoughtfully, "Boys, I wish you wouldn't do your sister that way." And that was all.

It was funny how she knew everything, almost.

We did get to go swimming in the pond that afternoon. From the first timid dip in the edge of the water where little frogs sprang in ahead of us to the after-swimming spring water ritual, it was great fun. I had just learned to swim in some fashion—like a desperate puppy! It was fun to show off to Suzanne, even though she could go faster running in the water than I could swimming. I wasn't brave enough to swim in the deep water where the others were, but I was brave enough to put my head under water and listen to the weird "throb-throb" of the ram pumping water up to the house. It sounded like a heartbeat.

There were bulrushes around the edge of the pond. We picked them and braided them later to sew together in the form of small baskets or doll's hats. There were tiny minnows to catch in our hands and we'd giggle as they tickled our fingers. One shoreside tree had limbs stout enough we could use it as a drop-off and splash into the water.

After about an hour our hands and feet looked like prunes, blackberry-scratched prunes streaked with mud. But we were never ready to get out when Daddy blew his whistle.

When we left the pond, we trooped in a long dripping parade down to the spring where there was a good-sized rock. One at a time we stood on that rock while another poured a bucket of icy spring water over us. It was a matter of bravery to be the first one. The bigger ones competed energetically for the job of pouring. It was a good way to take out your resentment on someone—pour cold water on him and watch him squirm and shake! The purpose of this rinsing was to get the pond mud off our skin, but we made it into a cruel, icy game.

The coolness and excitement of an afternoon's swimming could only be equaled by the fun and anticipation surrounding a watermelon cutting. The time we cut a watermelon we had grown ourselves was the most exciting cutting of all.

We didn't mean to plant the watermelons. They came up as if the seeds had been mixed in with the squash or something. Since they did come up and were doing so well, we began looking forward to the juicy red, cool taste of ripe melon. We checked them for size every day.

As soon as the melons were any size at all, we began teasing to cut one, just not able to believe they wouldn't be red yet like the ones from Uncle Hugh's. Blackberry season passed, the last blackberry pie was eaten, and we began majoring in squash, okra, and beans. Still the watermelons were not ready, not even the biggest one sitting so temptingly in the corner of the garden. Just didn't thump right, Mamma said.

At last, though, the day came for the first melon to be picked. Someone put it in the spring to cool all day. Late in the afternoon we took forks, napkins, salt, and the big butcher knife down to the little flat picnic place around that big stone at the spring. Daddy didn't feel like going, but we promised to take him a piece of melon.

This was our very own watermelon, a rarity since Mamma said they were hard to grow and we always planted more sensible things. We were so eager to sink our teeth into cool, sweet, juicy melon we didn't notice Mamma was looking a little anxious. She still wasn't convinced it thumped just right—but it had to be ripe, of course!

Stan was selected to cut and, being very dramatic, he poised the knife over the wonderful, striped melon and held it for the longest time while he made a philosophical speech about "All waiting ends sometime."

We crowded close as the knife sliced in and the crack widened with a delicious snap. Then there was a hushed gasp all around. The melon was whitish green inside, like a cucumber. There wasn't even a tint of red. That was one time we literally tasted disappointment. The salt didn't make it taste a bit better.

Mamma sighed, "I think it's a citron." Then she said more brightly, "It will make delicious pickles and preserves."

"Anybody for a drink of cold water?" asked Stan, laying down his fork.

What majesty and wonder lived in the woods in summer! Huckleberries on low bushes, Carolina wrens' nests like little caves down in the leaves and pine straw, the brook chattering over tiny rapids or humming in deeper places. The brook was so special in summer. Where shiny-leaved laurel bushes shaded it, sunlight came through layers of leaves to make unbelievable circles on the sandy brook bottom. There didn't appear to be any circle patterns in the leaves when you looked up. Yet there they were on polished stones and sand under the rippling water, sunny discs wavering with the wind. Chasing crawfish, catching water lizards, collecting water-smooth stones in little piles, and then sitting on the brook's bank letting the delicious warmth of sunshine and leaf-covered ground bring circulation back into blue feet—that was summer with a capital S.

Of course sometimes we didn't settle for everyday fun. Sometimes Charles the inventor, Stanley the instigator, and Suzanne and I, devoted followers, found more exciting things to do, such as boat-building. The boys decided wading wasn't good enough. They wanted to float. Actually, the idea came to them, I think, when they saw a certain log. Even though it was much smaller than dugout canoes we'd seen in pictures, it would be perfect for the small pool between the big beech tree and Indian Spring. That pool was deep, but it wasn't very wide or very long. This dugout boat would be just the right size.

It took several days, several blisters, and even a cut or two to get it ready for christening. Mamma kept wanting to know what we'd been doing when she'd discover bruises and scrapes. But we were all very secretive. No use disappointing anyone if this boat didn't float.

Sometimes we got so involved in digging out the middle of that log we failed to hear Daddy's whistle until the second call. We always knew we were in for a lecture, but we had a good long run to figure out a plausible story.

Finally the day came when the boat looked ready to be launched. She looked a little clumsy when the boys slid her in. But she did float and only tipped to the left a very little. The boys flipped a penny to see who got the first ride. Suzanne and I asked to be first, but Stanley said he or Charles would try it first to see if it were safe. (I knew that was only an excuse!) Stanley won the flip, and he carefully stepped into the boat which was tied to a tree. He could barely sit down, and when he did, his knees were under his chin. We all cheered, and Charles untied the rope and began to pull the boat around the little pool, wading across the brook in a shallower place with his breeches turned up.

The boat was floating, but most of it was not on top of the water, just an inch or two clearance. Suddenly that inch diminished to nothing when Charles turned a corner too fast. Stanley

couldn't unfold fast enough and got doused. He came up laughing.

We decided Stanley was too big for the boat. Charles would be next. He was smaller around and shorter. The boat should carry him. He stepped in and sat down. Carefully, not to tip the boat, he peeped over the side to see where the water came to.

"You've got about two and a half inches," Stanley declared cheerfully. "You should have a good ride. Here goes!"

Charles put hands behind his head, leaned back as much as possible and took on a look of princely relaxation as Stan pulled the boat around the pool. But that didn't last long, either. When the boat tipped, Charles scrambled out, but not before taking a nice cool dunking.

So it was my turn, only I wasn't quite so eager anymore.

"Come on now; you're so light, she'll float like a champ. Hop in. You'll have no problem at all."

"You wanted to be first, remember?"

I remembered. But things were different then. The boat had been dry and bound for a successful voyage, albeit a small one. Now it was soggy and her left-handed limp looked a lot more left-handed than before. Charles twitched the rope impatiently. I climbed in, being so careful that I almost tipped the boat right to start with. I crouched, holding tightly to the splintery sides. Suzanne cheered and I squealed as I careened around the pool, faster than either of the boys had gone. In fact, the whole world turned into a ripply swirl of green, blue, sky and water with three big smiles mixed in. Then there was a sudden jar as the boat hit bottom and I stood up bubbling, shaking wet hair out of my eyes, and stumbled up the bank.

The boys pulled the boat out again and held it for Suzanne who got in happily with no persuasion and sat right down on the wet bottom. It kind of made me mad that she could be so brave. I almost looked forward to seeing her dunked. But it looked as if the boat had finally found the right occupant. We all took turns hauling Suzanne around on that little pool until we were dizzy. She sang and dipped her fingers in the water, now and then waving to us and laughing in happy triumph and pure enjoyment.

All this time Crusoe, Suzanne's faithful and loyal little dog, had been whimpering and running up and down along the brook bank. He hadn't minded seeing the rest of us get wet. That was all in fun. But this was his mistress. "It's okay, Crusoe," she

called, but he didn't believe her. Suddenly with a yelp he
jumped straight into Suzanne's lap, and the boat overturned,
giving Suzanne and Crusoe the best dunking of all. We couldn't
stop laughing. Suzanne hunted for her eyes and Crusoe looked
like a drenched rat. After that, since we were all wet anyway, we
jumped into the water and had a really good water fight while
Crusoe barked from the bank.

Another water escapade was much more successful and entirely less drenching. There was a little waterfall in Indian Brook.
It was just around the bend from where the water came sparkling out from the duskiness of Laurel House and just below
where the giant exposed root made a perfect place for sitting and
dabbling feet in the water. You could hear the fall almost as far
away as the cabin, and just to hear it made you thirsty. The moss
that covered the bank on the Indian Spring side was rich and
thick like the velvet carpet in a palace. There were miniature
flowers in the moss, star-like white ones and blue forget-me-
nots. Masses of green algae slickened the water slide and gave
the water a greenish tint as it spilled down, but it turned white
and frothy at the bottom.

Charles was sitting on the bank by the waterfall one day chewing thoughtfully on the edge of a sourwood leaf. Suzanne and I
were wading in the pool the waterfall made, trying to catch the
bubbles floating out from where the water splashed. Stanley had
gone over to get a drink at the spring. Charles threw the leaf
down suddenly and leaned forward, putting his hand in the fall
and making water back up and splash white over his thumb.

"I've got it!" he yelled jumping up.

I ran over to see what he'd gotten, thinking it was a lizard or
maybe even a fish. But he didn't have anything.

"Got what?" asked Stan coming along wiping his mouth with
the back of his hand.

"That wheel's the thing," said Charles just as if we all knew
what he was talking about. "That wheel in the old shed below
the house. You know, the one that's a center of a train wheel.
Remember?"

"Yeah. But what are you going to do with it?"

"Make a waterwheel."

All efforts for the next month went into building a waterwheel. It was just watching effort on Suzanne's and my part. The
only thing we really got to do was to rescue tin cans from the
trash. It took a long time to get enough because about the only

thing we ate from tin cans was sardines, and those cans weren't shaped right. But Mamma got some salmon one week and some sliced pineapple, and we were able to find some applesauce cans from the winter before in the buried trash by the back fence. Charles said it wouldn't matter that they were a little rusty already.

I couldn't imagine how the wheel would really work. My faith was bruised from the boat experience. But Charles was determined. You could see it in his eyes, in the set of his chin, and in the way he bit down on his tongue at one side of his mouth. Stanley helped as much as he could, but he was too big to be allowed to play in the woods all the time. Daddy kept thinking of things for him to do. Lots of times he'd say, "Get Charles to help you," but Stan would say, "Oh, I can do it by myself." Sometimes he wouldn't say anything; he would just do the chore alone.

When the waterwheel was finished and finally set on a stake driven deep into the mud and sand under the water, we sat on the bank and breathed carefully as if we might mess it up. It had been so hard to get it set where the water would hit it just right. Once Charles had even given the whole idea up, but Stanley had helped him figure out a new way to do it. And now Charles was confident as he removed a large stone and some packed dirt from the dam we'd made and let the water tumble down the waterfall like something alive and greedy.

We stood and screamed in glee as the water plummeted into one carefully cut and placed tin can and then another around the wheel. Each time a can was filled, its weight turned the wheel to the next can, and the first one dumped its water out as it went under. Soon the wheel was spinning rhythmically, and there was a peaceful splash-splash added to the little roar of the waterfall.

"It works; it really works!" I yelled.

"Why shouldn't it?" asked Charles. "You can do all kinds of things with water—you just have to know how."

But Charles was disappointed because he and Stanley could never figure any way to use the waterwheel's power for anything.

"What good was it anyway," grumbled Charles. "All that work and it won't *do* anything."

Daddy stood on the brook bank, hands behind his back, admiring the merry little waterwheel. He'd come in the evening glooms to see if we'd cleaned out the spring as he'd told us and was surprised to hear that waterwheel chuck-chuckling about its business.

"It's a good thing," he pronounced. "Maybe it won't do any-thing to change the world, but there's value in simply making things."

The waterwheel spun for a long time. I guess it was there until the next spring when a flood ripped it off the stake and lodged it downstream in a sharp turn of a clay bank.

Sometimes excitement came our way unasked and unex-pected. That's what happened the day that I was getting reindeer moss for my birdshell collection. The best reindeer moss grew in a kind of swampy place between the brook and where the bluff loomed steeply, casting an afternoon shadow. The others had come along to help me since they didn't have anything better to do at the moment.

Almost forgetting what we'd come for, we started pretending that we were in the Okefenokee Swamp and that there were alli-gators and crocodiles submerged in the black holes. We jumped from moss tuft to moss tuft, squealing every time our feet slipped. Because of all our noise, the hush that fell suddenly on us was extra ghostly. We stood still for a moment, each in his own precarious place, staring at the object of our sudden silence. Finally Stanley went over and touched a big, brown balloon-looking thing. It bounced sluggishly in the mud as he gave a little push. The size and the color of it were what made it so weird. Suzanne just barely could look over the top of it. It was no ordinary toy, no ordinary anything.

There had been a lot of talk around home about flying saucers and things, unidentified flying objects, also a lot of talk about how powerful the Russians were becoming after the war. Was this thing from outer space, or was it an ominous sign from the Russians? I looked behind me quickly as if expecting some weird human or inhuman thing to be creeping up on us.

"We'll take it home to show it to Mom and Dad," said Stan.

"Do you really think we ought to touch it?" I asked.

Charles snickered. "You don't think it's a bomb, do you?"

Stanley walked in front with the thing. Charles was right be-hind him, and Suzanne and I brought up the rear. We were walk-ing into each other's heels we were in such a hurry, but Stan kept saying slow down because the thing could pop if it ran into a limb or something sharp. A low-flying plane went over and I dared not look, yet I had to see if another "thing" were falling—and what if it *were* a bomb?

Daddy looked at the balloon with great interest but no fear. He made us show him where we'd found it. Then he wrote to some official person, and in a few days there was a reply. Daddy asked Mamma to reread the letter to us at dinner that day. He could hardly keep from chuckling as he listened again.

But we who, though afraid of strange happenings, still longed to have them happen, who even wished a plane would crash on our place so we could rescue the people, were bitterly disappointed to find that the "thing" was only a weather balloon. It was a product of our own country for our own country!

When, in the middle of winter, I heard Daddy whistling "In the Good Ole Summertime," it made me think of a table heavy with steam-hot vegetables, cucumber sandwiches, and spring-cooled buttermilk. Or I'd think of picnics after church on Sundays or wiener roasts by moonlight with insect songs throbbing or maybe even frog legs for breakfast after the boys had a successful night on the pond. Thinking of summer made me remember the feel of warm earth under my feet or of the world turning upside down after I'd rolled sideways down Sunny Lawn. Or I'd remember climbing up Sunset Tree to get away from streams of warm milk the boys aimed at Suzanne and me as they did the evening milking. Finding a black snake in a hen's nest with a bump below his hideous head where he'd just swallowed an egg—that was summer. And certain trees, such as a dogwood with limbs drooping in every direction, or the red pine on Sand Flat, trees we almost lived in, were part of summer thoughts, too. Summer was capturing fireflies by the dozen and playing chase in the dew-damp grass until it was too dark to see whom you were chasing. And summer was—oh, yes—eating a green apple under a shielding forsythia bush with someone else eating one, too, sharing your guilt.

Chapter Five
The Season of...
Fall

The coming of fall meant the smell of apples cooking; it meant sourwoods turning red. They were the first trees to change color. Fall was whispered about among flocks of birds whirring from one tree to another in a close-to-earth rest stop. Fall was fingered by late butterflies resting briefly on clumps of beautiful weeds around the edges of the pasture. Fall meant school again.

"Why can't we go to public school like other children?" I complained, kicking the wood box with my new mail-order shoes.

"Because we want to teach you at home," Mamma said quite simply as she kneaded a batch of wheat bread dough.

"But why?"

Mamma thumped the dough hard and let it rest a minute as she looked at me. "Pat and Orman went to school for awhile when they were little," she said. "When the whole school closed down because of a measles epidemic, Daddy and I taught them at home to keep them up with their lessons. When Daddy realized how well they were doing and how much he was enjoying it, he wanted to keep on with it even after the epidemic was over. So he wrote the state superintendent's office for permission. And he got it."

"You mean he *wanted* to teach them? He *liked* it?"

"Yes. He likes teaching you, too. And so do I. But I'm sorry you can't have more friends. Friends are special, too. You'll see sometime, though, that this was best." That last was spoken more to a fist-sized dent in the dough than to me.

I ran my finger idly down a column of figures in my third-grade arithmetic book as I digested what she'd said. Even without putting my nose into that book I could have sniffed it from among several with my eyes blindfolded and hands behind my back. An arithmetic book never smells as good as a reader or a speller.

I was sitting on the iron stove's water warming tank. The warmth felt good and I had a nice view out the kitchen window to where some chickens scratched diligently. How nice it would be to be a chicken and not have to add and subtract.

"I don't like arithmetic," I said as if it were the first time. "Why do I have to study figures? No one would ever care if you just left that part off."

Mamma smiled. "You would. Someday." She gave the dough another round of beating that made the bin cover rattle. "If you learned only what you wanted to learn you'd be lopsided. Besides, how will you learn how to cook, sew, buy groceries, and especially how to play the piano if you don't know your arithmetic?"

"You mean you have to know arithmetic to play the piano?"

"Well, yes, to play in correct time you do."

That was the end of that (for the time being). I began working on my arithmetic with patient help from Mamma while she cooked. One of my sweetest dreams, born out of listening to music that made me ache deep inside, was to have a piano and to be able to play it.

There were many times when we thought the children who went to public school were so much more fortunate than we. They didn't have a grammar teacher around during all their waking hours. They didn't have a class that met in the study while supper was cooking fragrantly in the kitchen. And, best of all, they rode on a school bus.

But our friends were in classes of twenty and thirty children instead of two or three. We had all the help we ever asked for and then some. We had a simple system of family teaching in which we all learned by helping each other. Sometimes we didn't even realize we were in school! I learned the alphabet the spring before I started first grade while following Ginger back and forth on the garden trail.

Although school was wherever we were—in the kitchen, in the study, or on the big stone under the dogwood tree—one of the points of learning we most associated with school was the cabin in the south woods. There we had maps on the walls, books along the ledges, a couple of old-fashioned slates, a bench, a stool, and a desk chair Charles created himself. Sometimes we could just barely hear the traffic from the distant highway. Other than that there were only the varied bird calls, rustle of leaves, and the faint sound of tumbling water.

Daddy would come to discuss history, literature, and geography lessons which we were supposed already to have studied. We never knew exactly when he was coming. That's why the boys made an extra tiny window in the wall near the chimney, a peephole. An eye in that little crevice wouldn't be noticeable except at close range. A lookout would be set there whenever activities were less than studious, such as a game of marbles in session. The lookout could spot Daddy's helmet top the rise as he came up from Ramble Brook. He usually came whistling anyway, assuming we'd been studying unless it was proven otherwise. But, just in case, a lookout was good.

The cabin had burned once and been rebuilt by the older boys. For safety from the fire it now had a clay floor and clay walls up four feet from the ground with logs the rest of the way. There was a dusty, dry, clay smell mixed with wood smoke in all our books by the middle of January. It was a nice smell really.

One of the areas of learning I didn't recognize as school was Daddy's relaying of the news as he gleaned it from the radio (especially Morgan Beatty and H. V. Kaltenborn) and from the *Pathfinder*, a weekly magazine. He didn't really just relay the news; he commented on it at length during meals. We listened, not always because we wanted to, but because we knew better than to interrupt. Socialism was spreading over the world, Daddy said, threatening every thinking man's right to take care of his own family. We must realize the dangers in "something for nothing" and never be taken in by empty promises of politicians.

There was excitement over the whole house during the 1952 election, and no doubt was left as to who would make the best president. Eisenhower, Daddy said, had his faults, but he would make a good president if the scoundrelly democrats in Congress would let him.

"Eisenhower won't rob the rich who made their money with sweat and tears," he declared, "to pay the poor who could work if they would just get up out of their laziness."

When Eisenhower was inaugurated, the five of us children still at home went to town to see the ceremony on television. There was a crowd around every TV in stores on the square in Clarkesville. We finally found enough standing room around one in

Carey's general store. I sat down on the floor and peered between a man's legs to see. I shivered as the national anthem brought us all to our feet there in Carey's store smelling of coffee and cheese. The anthem was the best part to me. Of course it was interesting actually to see the president of the United States becoming president, lifting his arms, smiling so big, then soberly placing his hand on that Bible and taking the oath, saying, "I, Dwight David Eisenhower, do solemnly swear..."

Daddy was deeply concerned about soil conservation and tried to pass his concern on to us in every possible way. All of Pinedale was his laboratory and teaching hours were from dawn to dark. Trails were to be formed only in necessary routes; sticks and sawdust were laid systematically in bad washes. After storms hit, it was not uncommon to see someone binding a half-broken limb back against a tree with old rags. Those trees that were hopelessly damaged were cut down and used appropriately for saw timber or firewood. And always the branches were used for filling in gullies.

Family reading time from eight o'clock to ten o'clock every night was a treasured time. After we were ten years old, we were allowed to "stay up" and listen to Mamma read. Some days while hanging from a dogwood limb or racing down Sunny Lawn, I would suddenly remember that there would be more that night about poor little Oliver Twist or beautiful Lorna Doone. There was always something to look forward to.

Sometimes Mamma had to read pretty loud to be heard over a corn-shelling contest. Sometimes the boys whittled little boats and other shapes out of wood, scattering shavings around the fireplace. Usually the girls had sewing or knitting to do. It was hard for everyone to find a lighted place near the kerosene lamp, but after much scrambling, elbowing, and moving of chairs, we were ready to listen. I often sat on a stool at Mamma's feet. As the warmth of the fire toasted me and the rhythmic flow of Mamma's voice hypnotized me, even with a most exciting story like *Ivanhoe*, sleep often took over and her lap provided a soft landing place for my head.

Things were not always beautiful and easy in our schooling. Oh, no! Daddy's ultimatums often seemed so unfair, his demands so heavy. For example, one fall Stanley and Charles came up very short in a questioning about the French Revolution. (They had been making minibombs with matchstick powder and empty cartridge shells instead of studying. Those horrible little

things made enough noise to be heard clear to Hong Kong.)
Daddy was angry, furiously angry. He assigned each of them a
paper to write. He expected the essays to be read to him the next
afternoon. Charles was to write on events and conditions in
France before the revolution. Stanley was to cover the war itself
and the effects of it.

Charles was white with pent-up rage. After Daddy left Charles
said between his teeth, "I didn't study it in the first place because
it didn't make any sense. And I'm not going to study it now!"

He did try. Even late that afternoon when my lessons had long
since been finished, I found him still working on that paper. He
was at the foot of Sunny Lawn under the big red pine that was
like a giant wigwam. There was a pile of wadded first sentences
beside him, and he was staring at a picture of a guillotine in a
thick gray book. (History books always seem to be gray.)

"I can't do it!" he said, "I hate it! I don't want to know about
all that stuff!" He slammed the book shut and then snapped,
"What do you want anyway? To gloat over me because you
didn't have to write a stupid paper?"

"No. Mamma sent me to tell you about the bike…"

"The bike? What about it?" His face lit up.

"John's coming tonight to bring it. He said so in that letter today."

"What time?"

"After he gets off work, I guess. Why?"

"Oh, I just wondered. Have you got anything else to tell me?
I've got to study."

"No. Guess not. 'Cept Mamma said not to worry."

"Worry? Who's worrying? Now, go on, why don't you?"

It was funny how he changed so quickly. He still had to write
that paper, and he wouldn't be able to ride the bicycle until the
next afternoon. So how could he be quite so cheerful? But then
he *was* getting a bicycle, a brand-new bicycle, an early Christmas
present, and it would be there that night. If I were getting a bike,
I thought as I crawled under the pasture bars, I would be so excited even if there were a history paper still to write. After all, bi-
cycles in a family of ten children were very rare, bought only for
boys and then only when there was some special bargain somewhere.

I didn't think anymore about Charles and the history paper
(except to wonder a few times what color the bike would be) until about dusk when Mamma started calling him to come help

with the chores. There was no answer so she asked Stan to whistle through his fists for him. There was still no answer, just echoes. Daddy came out and blew Charles's signal with his little bottle once, twice, three times, but still there was no answer.

I ran unnoticed down to the red pine. There was hardly any trace that he'd been there. The pine needles were sort of ruffled, that was all. The wind was making eerie sounds in the top of the tree, and the echoing voices calling "Charlie! Char-lie!" sent a shiver up my spine. Where could he have gone? I thought he was over being mad, but maybe he wasn't.

When I got back to the house, Mamma and Suzanne were the only ones there. Daddy, Stanley, and Jackie were out with flashlights hunting and calling.

"What did Charles say when you told him about the bike?"

"Well, nothing much. He wanted to know what time John was coming. And he seemed real glad the bike was coming tonight."

"How was he coming on his paper?"

"Not very well. But he felt better about it after he heard about the bike. He told me to go on and leave him alone so he could study."

Mamma bit her lower lip as she strained milk through a cloth. "Where would he go?" she asked herself.

It must have been almost two hours before the others came back. Mamma had already served plates for Suzanne and me, and we had tried to eat. I was hanging around the kitchen door when Daddy came in the back and down the corridor. He was walking slowly and heavily. He didn't say anything as he took off his helmet and laid it on the breakfast room table. "He's not here, Eula," he said. "We've looked everywhere."

Mamma caught her breath, and Suzanne put her hands to her mouth.

"But wherever he is, he'll be back soon," I said confidently. "Because he wants to see the bike when it comes."

Daddy had started in the study but turned sharply. "The bike? He knew John was coming up from Atlanta tonight? Eula, do you think...?"

"I don't know; I just don't know." Mamma put her apron over her face and her shoulders began to heave. Daddy went to her quickly and put his arms around her.

"Now, don't cry," he said. "We'll find him. I'll send Stanley to a phone to call the state patrol."

Stanley went out the door, but he came right back in. "There's a car coming up the hill. Is it time for John?"

"No. He couldn't be here yet. He wasn't going to get off work before six o'clock, and he was going to his house before he came on up."

We went out on the front steps and watched the car lights bumping up the hill. It was a taxi. We could see the identification light on top. Thor and Crusoe barked furiously, and Daddy yelled at them to be quiet as he hurried over to the driver's window. We watched hopefully, but Charles didn't jump out. Daddy and the driver talked loudly to be heard over the motor that roared like a sawmill.

"Your daughter-in-law, Betty, called and asked me to come out and tell you your son Charles is there. He hitchhiked down. She said she would put him on a bus in the morning."

"Did she mention John?"

"Oh, yeah, he's on his way. Had already long left when the boy got there."

"Well, thank you for your trouble. How much do I owe you?"

"Have to get a dollar. You need to fix your road, you know that?"

"We like it the way it is," said Daddy curtly as he handed a dollar to the man.

When John came, Suzanne and I were in bed, but not asleep. I watched diamond shapes form on the ceiling as the car lights shone through our oriel window, and I wondered why Charles hadn't just waited.

"I wonder if Daddy will be very angry with Charles tomorrow," I said out loud.

"He will be, I bet," answered Suzanne. "I'm glad I'm not Charles right now, aren't you?"

"Yeah." Only I really wished Charles didn't have to be Charles right now, either.

Stanley, Jackie, Suzanne, and I met the bus the next morning. Charles kicked at stones all the way up to the house. He didn't want to talk at all. We showed him the bike, shiny and red, leaning against a garage wall. He whistled softly as he ran his hand over the front fender. Then the back door opened and he turned to face Daddy.

"Well, son, we're mighty glad to see you. Your mother and I have worried about you all night. What caused you to do such a foolish thing?"

"I don't know, sir."

"Well, I want to be sure it doesn't happen again! You understand?" Daddy lifted Charles's chin up with one hand so he could look him in the eyes.

"Yes, sir," Charles answered. The cowlick at the back of his head was vibrating.

"You really like the bicycle, don't you?" Daddy said, seemingly changing the subject.

"Oh, yes, sir!"

"But you will not ride it for two weeks. Do you understand that, son? Two weeks. Perhaps that will help you remember never to let this happen again." Daddy's mustache was twitching. He reached out as if to touch Charles's arm, but instead he turned sharply and walked back in the house, almost running into Mamma who was right behind him.

Mamma reached out impulsively and smoothed Charles's hair. "Come get something to eat," she said.

As I said, Daddy's ultimatums were hard. Charles still had to write that paper. And that bicycle, shining like new money, stood right there in the garage without moving for two whole weeks. Well, except for one time when Stanley put the kick stand up and just rolled it a few feet to be sure it wasn't rusting up or something.

It is true that some of us were "slicker" about getting around Daddy's instructions. For instance, John when he was a student at Pinedale's "university." He was always so interested in business deals, trading and selling almost from the time he owned anything. Many times when he was told to read a certain number of pages in a study book, he would turn the pages to the prescribed stopping place, slip through the woods, over the ridge, and into town to make a bicycle deal. He almost always got back to the cabin just in time to brush up on the subject and be ready for Daddy when he arrived. But if he did get caught (and the story is told that he was caught a time or two), he could always come up with a very reasonable story, such as having to drive a hunter from the place or rescue Charlie (that was before he had me tagging along) from a high tree on the ridge—or some such tale. He really was a clever talker, never telling a lie, just engaging in subject changes, I think. He even talked himself out of trouble the time he was gone all day, didn't even show up for lunch. Daddy ended up laughing and slapping him on his back, impressed by his business skill. He had bought a car for forty dollars.

The legend of John's skills was whispered amongst us, but as he would probably warn, "You have to know your limitations."

Every year the beginning of school held a certain excitement enhanced by the trip to the schoolhouse in town to get new books. If a book happened to be really new, that was grand. The new ones did smell so good. But used books were wonderful, too. It was such fun reading names of all the other children who had studied the books other years. Reading the names made you itch to write your own, too, in fancy letters like theirs. But Mamma said books were to be read, not written in, and it was an uncomfortable experience to have one's name discovered in the books.

Books were a very important part of our life. We were taught to respect them, to turn their pages carefully, and never to turn an opened book face down as that would break its binding. So it was really shocking when Daddy burned a book, a perfectly good, even new book. It was one someone had gotten for Christmas, but when Daddy discovered it was obscene, he called all of us together. As we stood jammed together in the kitchen, he opened the stove, ripped the book in half and stuffed it in. There were blue flames licking around the printed pages, eating them up as Daddy put the lid down and said, "Reading filth is as bad or worse than eating dung."

The beginning of school brought hope that this year math would make sense, English kings would arrange themselves in proper order, and smoke rings would curl off our pencils in writing class with the smoothness Mamma's did. Two weeks after the beginning of school, though, just as in all schools across the land, school was just school again. Then came September 17, my birthday, my own special holiday.

"I'm sure glad I don't go to public school," I thought as I sewed red sourwood leaves together with little sticks. "If I went to public school, I couldn't have a holiday on my birthday." I put my finished cap on my head and went to see if the grapes were getting ripe.

In the woods the leaves were falling in golden and red showers, making a rustling carpet on the ground. Squirrels worked under the hickory nut trees; holly and haw were loaded with red berries; and chips flew as Daddy cut stacks of firewood. Fall had come to Pinedale in all its glory. Mamma said to watch for the first shell flower to open by the brook and the first closed gen-

tian to point its way towards the sky.

You could smell grapes—muscadines, scuppernongs, and clusters of tiny, sour frost grapes. It was fun shaking the vines and picking up the grapes for Mamma and Jackie to make jelly. Charles liked the grape-hull pie Mamma made. It was too sour and sweet all at once for me.

After lessons each day, when we were small enough not to be too terribly useful in Pinedale's work force, we ran to play in the leaves, to build playhouses in a little circle of sourwood trees (with the help of mouthwash bottles and cracked cups), or maybe to lie on our backs in brown broom sedge watching the sky go over and knowing no one could tell where we were.

The maple tree at the back of the house turned purple and red and gold. It looked like a sunset or maybe a sunrise over the gray roof of the house. The sunset came to rest on the ground, and that was nice, too. It was also a little sad somehow.

One chilly morning we heard Daddy coming in the front door, clearing his throat. "There's snow on Old Tray today," he said.

We ran to look, Suzanne jumping up and down at the sight of the white covering on Tray Mountain which we could see through the mountain view Daddy kept clear. "I wish it were time for snow at our house!" she exclaimed. As we came back in, we heard Mamma and Daddy making plans for the day while Mamma washed breakfast dishes.

"Mr. Loggans will bring a wagonload of corn this morning," Daddy was saying. "The children can leave their lessons long enough to go and watch. The boys will need to help him unload."

It seemed Mr. Loggans would never come. He didn't come until we had already started arithmetic, but right in the middle of a long addition column, I heard the far-off rattle of the wagon wheels. Several of us ran down to the old barn where the corn would be stored.

Mr. Loggans tipped his hat "good morning" as he whoaed the mules. The wagon was piled high with harvest corn, the shucks brown with crisp curled edges. Suzanne and I watched as the boys used a giant scoop by turns unloading the wagon. We were fascinated by the quivering of the mules' wide nostrils as they snorted. Suzanne said they were trying to talk to us.

Mr. Loggans lifted us up into his wagon just to see what it was like before he left. "And this is for you little ones," he said with a wide smile all over his thin face as he turned a big orange pump-

kin so its best side was toward us. We ran our fingers down its
perfect seams. "Your mother can make some mighty fine pies
with that," he said.

We shyly said thank you and allowed ourselves to be lifted
back down, even though we would like to have jumped. Then
we waved as he maneuvered the mules back into the rough road.
The empty wagon rattled loudly as the mules "step-stepped"
down the road, around the bend, and out of sight.

That night there was a bright sunset behind the pines that
were beginning to sway in a cold, restless wind. Later the moon
came out, round and bright, making long white window shapes
across our quilt-covered bed. There was a ring around the moon,
though, Mamma said. "There will be a change of weather soon,"
she predicted as she tucked us in. "There! You're in bed right on
time tonight. Hear Morgan Beatty signing off the eight o'clock
news?"

"I bet it's going to snow," I told Suzanne, putting my cold feet
on the warm calves of her legs and delighting in her squeal.

"I hope it does," she said curling up in a tight ball. "I love the
snow."

But it didn't snow for a long time after that. It rained a little
the next day, the last rain we were to see for weeks. Daddy said
it was time to start raking a firebreak around the place. One afternoon as we were resting from the tedious job, we found a
road-sign fallen from its place on a tree near the highway.

The sign read "Grandma's Kitchen One Mile," and it was just
lying in the honeysuckle twenty feet from the road.

"It blew off this tree," said Stanley inspecting a resinous nail
hole.

"And it's on our land," said Charles turning the arrow-shaped
sign on edge. "It sure would make something nice."

"Like what? A sled?"

"Yeah! Or we could put wheels on it. We could use those
wheels from that old play wagon that's got only three. Three
would be just right for this."

"And then make a hole for a rope right in the point of the arrow, so we can pull each other around."

"Yessirree!"

"Let's get this thing back in the woods before anyone notices,"
said Stan. "Although I'm sure no one would care one iota about
this old sign. Grandma's Kitchen burned down months ago."

"But it's not ours," I spoke up. "What if the sheriff comes after us?"

"Aw, silly," Charles snorted. "The sheriff won't get us. Haven't you got any sense?"

"Well, what about Daddy?"

"Daddy won't ever know," said Stanley. "If it bothers you so, just remember you're not getting it. We are. Now run on back and start raking. And if you hear Mamma or Dad coming, whistle twice through your hands."

Wanting a part in the nice-sounding sled with wheels, I hushed and ran up to the top of the ridge and climbed back over the fence, an act which in itself was a misdemeanor (but it was such a long ways to the gate). Then I ran along the fence to the place where we had laid our rakes down. Suzanne was right behind me. I couldn't help remembering, as we began to rake again, the admonition, "Don't pick up things that fall beside the highway." Why, it was almost as strong a commandment as, "Don't sit on the ground when it's damp." "Those things don't belong to you," Mamma would say, "and anyway they're filthy dirty."

I stopped suddenly in the leaves and Suzanne did, too. "I wanted to hear if anyone else is coming," I said breathlessly.

But the sound I had heard was only Thor walking through the leaves hunting a rabbit's trail.

"Do you think we'll get caught?" Suzanne asked with her big brown eyes bigger than ever under her bangs.

"I hope not," I said.

"What if Daddy comes before the boys get back?"

"Uh, well, I guess we could say they're gone for a drink of water. They will be coming from the direction of the spring when they come back from hiding that thing near the cabin."

"Well, that's a lie," said Suzanne judiciously.

"What else can we say? Anyway, maybe they will get a drink of water."

I began to rake furiously and soon had new blisters on my hands. The firebreak was to be about fifteen feet wide and was to go all the way around Pinedale's woven wire fence. The fifteen feet, of course, was not exact. We measured by trees: the clean raked surface with earthworms squirming where they were uprooted was to reach this tree here and that one there. There was a certain enjoyment in the yearly task of getting ready for the fall drought—seeing the firebreak stretch out behind you and noting how neat and straight your section was. We took pride, too, in seeing how our sections blended together so it looked as if one person had done it all.

We didn't have to tell a lie that time. Stanley gave an admiring whistle when he came back and saw how much we'd raked. "We ought to sneak off more often," he teased.

Somehow that Saturday the boys found time to build the sled. Suzanne and I were kept busy at the house that day. But that night when we were going to bed, I heard the boys talking in their room. "Isn't she a beauty?" one of them exclaimed to the other who answered, "We'll try it out tomorrow afternoon."

All through the Sunday afternoon service my eyes kept drifting sideways to be sure Stanley and Charles didn't slip out without my knowing it. This was one of my favorite times of the week when we sang together out of Mamma's yellowed hymnbook and then listened while she read to us from her Bible that was full of pictures. But it was all lost on me that day.

When we finally left the house, it was as if we had all four been shot from a cannon. The door wasn't big enough to let us out. Jackie ran out after us, but she stopped at the pasture wall and watched us run down Sunny Lawn and disappear up Tulip Hill. I knew she wished she weren't grown up already.

When they were hidden from the house, the boys slowed down. Charles looked over his shoulder and glowered at me. "You didn't want any part of this thing. What makes you think you're going to ride on it?"

"You want me to go tell Daddy on you?" I threatened.

"Oh, now, y'all stop it," said Stanley. "Of course she can ride. Don't you remember how hard she raked?"

"Well, it's not fair," grumbled Charles.

"It is, too!" I said furiously. "And what about Suzanne? She didn't help you, either."

"No, but she's the baby," said Charles, his slender face softening as he looked back at Suzanne.

We walked on in silence to the pine thicket on the other side of Tulip Hill. The air between us suddenly cleared. There was the sign with three wheels now, pointing itself along a natural street between two rows of pines, the only pines on the place planted in rows. It really didn't look like a sign anymore. Suzanne had a turn first, and she laughed with pleasure as she blinked between the trees. Then it was my turn, and I held tightly to the board as Charles took off at full speed, turning curves recklessly, curves

that I couldn't prepare for because he was engineering them as he went!

Sometimes it seemed as if a tree were coming straight towards me, but just as I'd be getting ready to roll off in self-preservation, Charles would turn and we'd skitter past. "Hold on!" he kept yelling which he didn't need to do because I was already holding on until my arms ached.

The boys gave each other turns and strange trails began to appear in the thicket where the needle carpet had been so smooth. We hardly noticed them ourselves, such fun we were having. The sled really was fast, and we decided to name it "Lightning." One time in turning a curve too fast, it slid into a pine brush wigwam we had built some Sundays before. That would have been all right except that some wasps had chosen the wigwam for their home, and they reacted violently to being so rudely disturbed. We had to abandon that side of the thicket!

We hardly noticed that the sun had drifted very low and now made our leg shadows long across the ground and that the air was getting cooler as evening approached. Even if we had noticed we might not have thought about how Daddy and Mamma liked to go out strolling that time of day. We were having so much fun.

Stanley was pulling Charles on a crazy trail that wound in and out of the rows of trees. They were both yelling, and Suzanne and I were cheering when suddenly there were Mamma and Daddy walking toward us. They were smiling to see us having fun, but my knees began shaking. Suzanne twisted a corner of her dress hem up and began sucking it. The boys didn't see Mamma and Daddy until they started back along their zig-zag trail. Then they stopped suddenly, Stanley dropping the rope and Charles stretching out his legs to cover the bright red letters on the arrow-shaped platform.

"You're playing entirely too roughly for Sunday," said Daddy, but you could tell he wasn't going to be upset about it this time. "You'll have to rake pine needles back over these naked areas. We don't want a wash through here." All this time he was walking casually towards Charles who was still hugging the sled. "What kind of an invention have you made now, boys?"

Seeing the machine-cut arrow point which Charles was unable to hide, Daddy's jaw suddenly went hard and he stopped as if slamming against a wall. Jerkily he whisked Charles off the sled and stood back up, hands fisted, glaring at that sign.

It really was a sign again. It said "Grandma's Kitchen One Mile" just as plain as day, and it looked ridiculous with wheels on it and that rope attached to its arrow. I clenched my own hands in tight knots.

"Whose idea was this?" Daddy asked sternly while the blood began to rise to his face.

"We found it buried in honeysuckle over beside the highway," said Stanley.

"It was twenty feet back," added Charles hopefully.

"Yes, at least twenty feet," agreed Stanley, putting his hands in his pockets and rattling some screws and things.

Daddy exploded. "Don't you know this doesn't belong to you?" he shouted, pointing at Stanley with a sharp finger and waving his helmet at the sign with his other hand. "What possessed you to do a thing like this? And when did you find the time? Did you build this thing on Sunday, too?" His shouting got louder and louder, and I wanted to put my fingers in my ears, but I was afraid to move for fear I would be noticed.

Suddenly there was an electric silence. Daddy put his hand to his forehead and then quickly put his helmet back on. "First thing in the morning," he said in a repressed quietness, "I want this thing dismantled and taken back where it came from. Do you hear?" ("Yes, sir. Yes, sir," from Stanley and Charles.) "Or better still, nail it back up where it originally belonged and be sure it's in the highway right-of-way. I don't want this on my place." Almost under his breath he said, "Signs! Everywhere! Cluttering up the beauty of the land! Beer joint signs! Abominations!"

"Yes, sir," said Stanley and Charles together when they thought he was through.

"Don't ever let me find you desecrating the Sabbath day with stolen goods again!" said Daddy, and he abruptly started towards the house.

Mamma looked sad as she stroked Suzanne's hair. She started to say something a couple of times and stopped. Finally as she turned away, she said softly, "Come in pretty soon, children."

After they were gone I relaxed my hands. "Why didn't you tell him I was part of it, too?" I asked.

"There wasn't any need for that. We were responsible," said Stanley sliding to a sitting position beside a tree. He nursed a sore thumb as if suddenly that were more important than anything.

"Actually, we didn't have a chance to," said Charles. "But anyway, you're too little to count."

Soon, with a backward look at the wonderful sled that had ridden us so gloriously, we started home. I wondered which was worse—to be included in the prank and suffer from the blaze of Daddy's eyes or to be considered "too little to count."

It was October, 1950, and the worst drought in years hung onto the North Georgia hills. Everything was thirsty. Forest fires were breaking out all around us; there was danger from the tiniest careless spark. Daddy sent Charles and me with books and Suzanne with her doll Julia over to the south woods. "If you see signs of fire anywhere near, let us know immediately," he said.

The sun was so dimmed by smoke that you could look it in the eye without blinking. You could actually see the air because it was yellow and thick. It was threatening with the taste of ashes. We tried to study, but it was hard to keep our minds on our books with such an ugly, foreboding silence around us. The birds weren't even singing.

We climbed the Bluff and "made camp" around the tallest pine called Blue Ridge, the one the boys used for lookouts. They had nailed boards ladder-fashion up the trunk to the lowest limb so they could scoot up in a hurry. The Bluff was the very steep end of a long ridge and was one of the highest points on the place. By climbing Blue Ridge on a clear day a person could see far and wide. That's what the boys said. They even declared they could see a faint range of the Smokies. Eying the "steps," I sometimes wondered if I couldn't make the climb myself. But when I'd try, my legs just couldn't reach. The boys could have put them closer together, but they didn't.

Not far down the hill from Blue Ridge was a big rotten stump, hollowed out with time. Suzanne and I played for awhile around it. The crumbly dry rot on the floor of it was almost griddle warm under our feet as we climbed in and out an imaginary door. Then we settled down under a sourwood tree, not far from the neatly raked firebreak by the fence, within a few feet of Blue Ridge's stalwart trunk.

I watched a grandaddy longlegs spider move along, up and down, over the dry leaves that were mountains to him. As I watched, I chewed the edge of a sourwood leaf. Suzanne was playing with Julia. Julia was all plastic, but she was as real to Suzanne as the baby who had visited us the Sunday before and whom Suzanne had been allowed to hold.

We were startled when Charles yelled from about twenty feet up Blue Ridge in a voice of utter horror, "Look! Look at that stump!"

My throat tightened and the scream I wanted to make didn't come. The stump where we had played minutes before was a pillar of fire with sparks shooting up into the trees like millions of upside-down shooting stars. Charles must have touched only every third board coming down that tree, or maybe he just leaped. Anyway, we all three ran towards the fire, Charles ripping a green bough from the sourwood as he went.

"Run! Run to the house!" Charles urged. "Quick! run!"

With that one word, "Run!" in my mind I started off like a machine. There was energy in me that wasn't really mine. Suzanne followed right behind me as I tumbled and slid down the Bluff, not the easy way, but straight down the steepest part. Because that seemed quickest. Even the hazelnut bushes that had been so kind to share with us were thick and painful to run through. We didn't pause for air as we sped around Indian Spring or when we passed the cabin. We leaped across Ramble Brook, so dry now there were no trickles anywhere and ferns were curled tight on the banks. With no sound in my ears but Suzanne's footsteps pounding sturdily behind me and Charles's words playing over and over, I thudded around Tulip Hill's thicketed side and past the treehouse calmly looking out through oak branches as if nothing were unusual. The slope of Sunny Lawn looked so high, so steep. I didn't believe I could climb it, but I saw this horrible picture of fire licking up into the trees and Charles all by himself beating at it with that sourwood limb. The next thing I knew I was heaving myself over the stone wall at the top of the pasture, pushing on up to the house with nothing but sponge in my legs, and finally stumbling down the corridor, collapsing outside the kitchen door.

Dad was talking to Mamma and Jackie as they cooked dinner. He held his hands behind his back and strode back and forth between the kitchen and his study talking politics and my mind worked desperately to get my mouth to shout, but nothing would come out. I'd run all this way and now couldn't even get out "Help!"

"What is it, Brandy Brew?" Dad asked, sitting down beside me when he heard me moan. He shook me a little and lifted my trembling chin. "What – is – it? What's wrong, girl?"

"Fire! The woods!" I whispered only faintly but he heard me. Dad alerted Mamma and Jackie as he reached for his helmet. Then he said to me, "Go on to Hackett Hill. Stan is there watching the cow. Tell him to go to the woods immediately. Can you go that far?" I nodded numbly and left, this time all alone, for Suzanne was in a heap on the stone seat. Her four-year-old legs wouldn't go any farther. Mine were so weak they kept running into each other, but somehow they carried me to Hackett Hill.

Stan left me with the cow and ran off so quickly it seemed as if he hadn't even been there. But there was the comfortable place in the honeysuckle where he had been lying. His civics book was still there, open to the qualifications of senators.

Scamp, the cow, wanted to go to the highway instead of home. I struggled and tugged, wheedled and coaxed her as far as our driveway, but there she insisted on turning towards the highway instead of back to her own pasture. As she and I engaged in a tug-o'-war beside the Old Entrance curve, cars began to come. The drivers were strangers to me, carload after carload of them. Their faces were set and they didn't even notice the cow and me in the honeysuckle. I was glad. It was terrifying to see that many cars in our usually very quiet driveway.

When I finally got Scamp in the pasture and got back to the house, I found Suzanne huddled on a chair by the kitchen stove crying and shaking.

"Jackie said watch the cookies," she sobbed. "They're gone to fight the f-f-fire. Oh, poor little Julia!" she cried. I suddenly felt very sick at my stomach.

The cookies were dismally charred and my own tears came spilling over as I stood in the middle of the floor holding the pitiful pan, wondering what to do with that mess. A feeling of dread settled in us like rough heavy stones. It was bad enough for men to fight the fire, but Mamma should be here in the kitchen where she always, always was. She might fall over some brush or get her thick hair on fire. And Daddy wasn't supposed to be so active either. He might have a heart attack or another heat stroke.

We stayed right there in the kitchen seeking security in the familiarity of a sleepy cat in the woodbox and an iron kettle full of simmering beans. That is, we stayed there after we buried the burned cookies out back under a hemlock tree. It seemed the best thing to do with something so dreadfully dead.

It seemed like several years before we heard tired footsteps approaching the back door. Mamma and Jackie were back. The way they walked I knew their legs felt like mine. Hair stuck to their sweaty faces and Mamma's nose was very red. They both held their hands out from them as if they were trying not to get dirt on their clothes, but their dresses were smudged with black already.

Mamma managed a note of cheer. "Everything's all right! They'll soon have the fire put out." She hugged us both and smoothed Suzanne's hair with the back of one hand.

"Did you bring Julia?" asked Suzanne holding tightly to Mamma's skirt.

Mamma looked stricken and I turned my head. "We'll get you another doll, Honey," she said.

Suzanne cried herself to sleep in Mamma's arms while Jackie prepared a bucket of dinner for the boys. Mamma said take all we had and share with any of the men who would stay. But as Jackie and I walked to the woods with the food we met streams of cars again. The fire was under control and the men were leaving. This time they nodded, some even spoke out open windows. Our place had been saved and a potential forest fire stopped. They were all very glad, no matter how tired they were.

The Bluff was black now with an ugly red glow around edges of stumps and up the sides of trees. All the deep, rustling leaves were ashes, as were the hazelnut bushes, the wren's nest near a big oak tree, the sourwood, the grandaddy longlegs, and Julia. Daddy and the boys were watching the edges of the burned area to be sure no sparks started new fires. At the sight of dinner, their smudged faces relaxed a little. It was almost three o'clock and they were starved.

Jackie began unloading the bucket beside Indian Brook where a patch of moss under laurel bushes was still green. We all flopped down except Daddy. He seemed to have a spring inside him wound up tight, and he couldn't stop walking back and forth.

"I've never before known a stump spontaneously to combust," he said as he puzzled. "But that's the only answer here. Hope fire doesn't burst forth elsewhere. Anyway, you did a mighty good job of watching out, Charlie Boy, and you all did well in fighting fire." He paused by Charles who looked up and said, "Brenda was the one who ran so far."

"That's right, she did," said Daddy, suddenly remembering me. "How are your feet, Brandy Brew?" he asked.

I hadn't thought about my feet and looked down at them

quickly. Daddy laughed as he took the dish of beans and potatoes Jackie offered him. It was the last time he would laugh for
awhile. The crisis was over, but the hard work of conserving the
burned soil, cutting burned timber, and replanting trees was not.
Two days later the rain came.

Thanksgiving Day dawned differently from ordinary days. It
was supremely wonderful because you knew as you first woke
that there would be no lessons that day. You'd snuggle down in
the covers with a fight going on inside you, whether to sleep
some more while you could or to jump into some clothes and
run to do the things you were always wanting to do, like climbing trees or making villages.

The fight would soon be won for me by Suzanne who would
punch me in the ribs and say, "I smell something good! Aren't
you going to get up, goose?" (Goose was her favorite nickname
for me, not just at Thanksgiving.)

On Thanksgiving Day the sun was bigger and redder than on
other days. And it was always there because it never rained on
Thanksgiving. If it had, how could we have taken our dinner to
the south woods for a picnic every time for so many years?

The very trees seemed thankful to God on Thanksgiving if
only for the freedom to feel breezes up where people couldn't
reach. As I ran out before breakfast with Suzanne to see about
her dogs, I'd hear the trees talking, low and humming-like.
When I looked up far into their tops where the sunshine was
bright, I wished that for just a minute I could be one of the birds
that flew to a tree just to sing a song. Suzanne didn't need to be a
bird to sing. She hauled herself onto the stump of a big oak
which had been cut to give the hemlocks more room. Standing
there with her arms open wide, she sang. "Oh, what a beautiful
morning, Oh, what a beautiful day..." Then she laughed as she
leaped off that stump, startling a cluster of chickens out of their
early morning dust bath. Her legs twinkled from under her pina-
fore dress as she raced Crusoe around the house. "Come on,
Goose," she yelled happily.

Breakfast was extra good with no forebodings of arithmetic
ahead. Everyone was full of big plans for the day—everyone, including Daddy, who said as he ate eggs, cornmeal mush, and hot
bread, "Since you don't have lessons today, boys, let's do some
cutting in the woods. There are a few small trees over in Turtle
Hollow that need taking out."

Charles heaved a big can't-win-for-losing sigh. He and Stanley had been planning to fix a broken chain on the bicycle. But they didn't complain in words; you could just see their disappointment in the way they slowed down eating, took smaller bites.

Daddy saw it, too, I guess. "We won't work all day," he assured them, "you'll have some time for target practice—or following the streams. Maybe while you're running around you can even give the fences a good checking before the day's done."

The boys exchanged glances and I knew they were hoping Daddy wasn't going to work with them today. But Daddy picked up his helmet before Charlie had swallowed his last bit of cocoa.

"We'll bring dinner to the woods and meet you all at Indian Spring," Mamma called after the boys. "And now, you girls can help prepare dinner."

We looked behind us, sure she was talking to Jackie and Ginger. But of course they already knew they were helping with dinner. No, she meant we little girls could help. Suzanne and I looked longingly at the carpet of many-colored leaves under the maple tree. We could have such a nice playhouse there. But Mamma said we were big enough to peel oranges and crack nuts for the fruit salad.

Being big enough to help was really pretty nice. With Thanksgiving music pouring from the radio and with the smell of pumpkin pies everywhere, it was really fun to have a part in making Mamma's huge fruit salad. The sounds, smells, sights, all were so rich—even the feel of the fruit made me tingle with a kind of thankful excitement. Oranges were rare except for very special occasions as were nuts other than hickory.

Thanksgiving morning passed more quickly than others, even though it was longer. It took until one o'clock for the chicken and dressing, pies, turnip greens, and everything else to cook. Then we all loaded up with pots and pans and buckets of wonderful smelling food and started to the woods. Even though I was hungry, I felt already full just from smelling all the good things for so long.

Sometimes at Thanksgiving there were bright leaves still on King Tulip, on the sweetgum trees, and on other trees on The Island. We called it The Island because there was pasture grass like a green lake all around that one big cluster of hardwoods. Down the middle of the "island" flowed a trickling spring with a weeping willow draped tenderly on one bank.

But fall was faster some years and the leaves would have already fallen completely when we made our Thanksgiving trek. Leaves then would lie thick over the spring so that, if you didn't know better, you'd walk into the water. Mamma said Orman and Brantley had tricked Aunt Dee that way one time, helping her over the wrong place and then purposely letting her step right in the leaf-covered water!

At Apple Bars, instead of sliding heavy poles back for an opening in the fence, we climbed over, under, or through bearing our burdens of food. No matter how awkward, that seemed the easier way, the bars were so heavy to maneuver. Beside the gate scarlet fronds of sumac fanned, gently brushing the rough trunk of a pine. On the other side of the fence the fallen leaves were much thicker and rustlier and there was a deep nutty scent in the south woods you never found anywhere else.

As we went past the cabin and approached Indian Spring, Jackie halloed as she was proud of being able to do, somewhat like a Swiss yodeler, and there was a quick anguished answer from one of the boys. They came running to meet us, peeping into the pots, almost eating the food with their eyes, though they knew well not to grab any prematurely. Crusoe, taking them for an example, promptly sat up and begged right there in the trail.

Our picnic was beside the spring, a wide sparkling pool contained within mossy, fern-grown banks, and approached by a little one-person flight of stone steps. There was a legendary story Daddy referred to about how the Indians laid flagstones in the bottom of the spring and some of us aspired to dig sometime until we found those flagstones. Daddy said the townsfolk used to come out in wagons and buggies to picnic right here where we did now and there were ancient ruts around the end of the Bluff. The Three Sisters (towering great tulip trees) clustered around a smaller spring separated only by a narrow mossy "bridge." That spring we called Indian Children's Spring. Between the brook and the springs were two oak trees standing close together like chatting friends. Daddy had jammed a board between them, maybe right after he and Mamma married, making a nice woodsy seat for her. Now the trees had grown together over the board until they were almost one. We pleaded with Mamma to sit there if only for a minute and she blushed when Daddy called her his queen.

We picked sticks out from under the blue flowered tablecloth so it wouldn't be bumpy for pots and pans. In a hush filled with the innocent noise of Indian Brook, the songs of birds, even the

rustle of a bug crawling over a dry leaf, Daddy gave thanks to
God for our food and our life and for the majesty of so great a
Creator. He also took time in his prayer to thank God for our
country and to ask Him to keep us strong in spite of ourselves. I
felt a reverence too big for me to understand, even though at the
same time I was holding my stomach tightly trying to keep it
from growling out loud.

As big as the cracked enamel pot was, and as big as the
smoked camper cooker was, and as big as Mamma's new alumi-
num pots were, there wasn't much left in any of them to carry
back. Daddy laughed and said we were like a bunch of wild
things gnawing the charred carcasses of fellow creatures (meaning the chickens).

After dinner Dad lay on his back on the ground, his head in
his hands, and talked philosophically of the beginning of
Thanksgiving, the present political situation, and the fact that in
just one year the Bluff had been restored miraculously from its
bad burning. Charles, Suzanne, and I left the grown-ups talking
and began chasing each other back and forth across the brook.
We chased each other on the big tulip log bridge high above the
little waterfall, sometimes on mossy stepping stones, sometimes
in flying leaps shore to shore, or even balancing on a great
crooked root that formed a low bridge across a pool. Tiring of
that game, we applied our chasing ability to capturing slippery
minnows, then warmed chilled hands on sunny, soft moss
patches. As we played and the older ones talked and likely en-
vied us, shiny laurel leaves made the sunshine touchable and the
smell of crushed sweet fern was very pleasant.

Pat, Orman, Brantley, John, and later Ginger all came home for
Thanksgiving whenever work schedules, school, and long miles
allowed. After they had families of their own to bring to Pinedale for Thanksgiving visits, the dinner changed. It became a
five o'clock dinner in the Hall with everyone dressed in Sunday
clothes and with fire in both fireplaces. Both leaves would be
pulled out on the dining table, and the buffet glowed with
pumpkin and mincemeat pies. Daddy, in his suit, beamed
around at everyone with great pride. We made quite a big circle.
As we bowed our heads, he gave thanks for another year with all
its blessings and for a country founded on liberty for all.

There was one bad thing about Thanksgiving—the dirty
dishes. Mamma could gather up a good many on any day, but on
Thanksgiving the dishpan had to be filled and refilled because

the water got cold before the dishes were done. Outside the
kitchen window, the dogwood tree was in shadow except for the
very top where the sun, sinking in the west, could still reach it
over the roof of the house. I hurried to finish my part in the
washing, rinsing, and drying assembly line so that I could run
with Suzanne down Sunny Lawn and up Tulip Hill to watch the
sunset from Sunset Tree.

Thanksgiving Day left much faster than it came. Suzanne and I
had just warmed up our bed so that we could stretch out our
legs into warm caves when she suddenly sat bolt upright letting
the cold rush in around us.

"Lie down, you're freezing me!" I complained.

"I just thought of something," she said breathlessly.

"Well, what is it?"

"We're one day closer to Christmas. It's only twenty-seven
more days."

Chapter Six
The Season of...
Winter

The dreariness of winter didn't come until after Christmas. Cold days came. Heavy frosts came. Water in the cedar bucket on the kitchen cabinet iced over as did all the puddles in the road. We would have to run and stamp our feet to keep them warm as we watched the beautiful holly tree to be sure no trespassers brutally pruned it for seasonal decorations. The holly tree was not very far from the highway, easily accessible, and Daddy couldn't bear the thought of its being "undressed" by anything but the birds. Mamma was allowed only a few small branches for her own decorations.

Before Christmas the days were so electrified with excitement that the cold just didn't matter. We blew warm breath on our mittened fingers and went on playing or working. There was a lot of work to be done before Christmas. Especially that year the boys built the little house.

We had worked together on the little house all fall, the four of us. But when the outside was finished from the door latch (made of inner tube rubber) to the shingled roof (shingles the boys had split themselves), Suzanne and I were told we couldn't help anymore.

"This is our workshop," Stanley said. "And it's getting close to Christmas. We might have some secrets."

We were deeply disappointed that we couldn't go inside the cute little house anymore and just when it really became most interesting. But the idea of secrets for Christmas was so exciting, we couldn't complain. We found a secret hiding place of our own behind a big rock above Ramble Brook. We made tiny cups and bowls from clay we dug out of the brook banks, collected beautiful pebbles, made clay leaf prints, and painted little acorn faces. But none of these were appropriate for our brothers.

We examined the "fruit" of the woods for something that could be made into a really wonderful present: long, slender, white pine cones, red twin berries on the squaw vine, nice wide slabs of bark from a yellow pine, even sheets of "paper" from a huge rotting tulip log. But there was nothing just right for fashioning something that would make Stanley and Charles say, "Hey, look at *this*!"

As we listened at a close distance to the hammer and saw sounds in the little house, we worried. What *could* we make for them? We finally went to Mamma for help and learned how to hem handkerchiefs. Even that wasn't completely satisfying, though, since we knew very well what happens to boys' handkerchiefs.

Christmas really began when Pat and Ginger came home for the holidays smelling of tobacco smoke because of the long bus rides from their different schools. We shared our secrets and our worries with them and they, just as Jackie had done, said, "Don't worry. Everything will be just fine. They'll love their handkerchiefs." They took us to Clarkesville to see Santa Claus and to see the reindeer "flying" over the Reeves Building. Santa Claus had a very nice and merry "ho, ho, ho," and I liked the candy he gave me. As we left, I kept looking back at him trying to figure out who he really was. Could have been the Sunday school superintendent, I decided.

Finally, after what seemed to be centuries, Christmas Eve came. We were so glad that at our house we opened presents the night before Christmas and didn't have to wait until morning. One more night of curiosity and we might pop. The reason for having Christmas early was because of a compromise between Mamma and Daddy. At Daddy's home the family had opened gifts on Christmas Eve night. In Mamma's family the opening of presents was on Christmas morning. Like Daddy's family, we opened Christmas presents on Christmas Eve. Then, on New Year's Eve, we hung stockings and got up at the crack of dawn next morning to see what was in them. We had both Mamma's and Daddy's Christmas traditions twined colorfully into one of our very own.

On that Christmas Eve the big girls suggested that we all walk to the south woods while Mamma and Daddy dressed the tree. It was traditional that the children not see the tree until it was decorated, with packages under it ready to be passed out by Daddy. I objected to leaving, not wanting to be too far from the scene of excitement, but Pat said the stars were so bright that you just couldn't tell what you might see on a night like this. "Besides," she said, "John isn't home from work, and we may have a long wait. Might as well have a good, brisk walk."

The cold wind stung our noses and ears as we walked. Jackie and the boys went ahead of us, but we didn't think anything about it. Ginger and Pat told us stories, one right after another. As we crested the last little hill before reaching the cabin, we gasped in surprise, interrupting an almost-convincing story of Santa Claus and his elves.

"Why, there's a light in the boy's workshop!" said Pat excitedly. "It must be the elves at work right now. Do you think?"

Suzanne and I began to run, leaving the flashlight behind us. It wasn't the elves at work, but maybe we would be allowed to see whatever it was the boys had worked so hard on. We were out of breath both from excitement and running so hard when we arrived at the little house where a candle's light was haloed in the one tiny window.

The others were there standing outside stamping their feet and blowing on their hands. "Go on in," said Charles eagerly. "Go on. It's all right." We could hardly believe it. Was this a trick?

I sucked in my breath so hard when I saw what was inside that it made my throat burn. The little house had curtains on the window and pictures on blue wall-papered walls. There was a round wood table just the right size for doll tea parties with a vase of paper flowers on it. In the corner was a doll's bed made from two worn-out batteries put together and covered with a quilt. There was even a hooked rug on the floor and a little bench to sit on.

We touched each thing slowly and reverently, not believing what we saw. Suzanne took a plate out of a little dish cabinet and set it lovingly on the table.

"Just think! You can play in it tomorrow all day!" Jackie said. (She had made the rug and curtains, we learned later.)

"We're going to play right now, aren't we, Goose? Sit down and I'll make you some tea."

The others standing outside sang "Jingle Bells" so crisply and clearly and it was the merriest thing that ever had happened. Then Pat stuck her head in the door. "Guess we better go now,"

she said. "Mom and Dad will have the tree trimmed soon, and we don't want to be late. John might be there by now, too. Oh, I wish Orman and Brantley could be here, too. But you two put your tea things away, save 'em for another day. This is just the nicest playhouse I ever, ever saw."

We thought so, too.

As we walked home Pat started singing "O, Little Town of Bethlehem," and we all joined in. When I turned my head back and looked up at the stars with my eyes squinted a little, I could almost see the Christmas tree. I was so excited, I wondered why my body didn't lift off the ground at least several feet. But there was one thing wrong which kept me earthbound, I guess. I was worried about those handkerchiefs. If only we could have done something as nice for our brothers as they had done for us. We waited in the kitchen and storeroom for the blast of the trumpet that would mean "Come to the Christmas tree!" Charles was on top of the bags of wheat in the storeroom keeping watch for the glow of the first candle on the tree. We weren't supposed to climb on the wheat, but at Christmas it was different. Only from so high a place, looking though the open kitchen shelves, could one see the light shine through the high translucent window between the kitchen and stairs and Hall.

"If you don't eat any supper, you can't eat candy and oranges later," said Pat, still trying to interest us in roast beef, baked sweet potatoes, and green beans.

I wanted candy and oranges later. But there was something so big in my stomach already, I just couldn't swallow any supper. Suzanne and I kept punching each other and passing ecstatic comments about our perfect playhouse. Yet there was more excitement coming: The Christmas Tree!

"He's going to blow it in a minute now," said Stanley coming back in the kitchen from the corridor.

"How do you know?" asked Jackie suspiciously.

"I just know."

"You peeked!" accused Ginger.

Just then Charles yelled out, "I see it! They're lighting the candles!"

I almost pulled a bag of wheat down on myself climbing up to look at the warm little halos in the window, and then I came back down even faster to be sure I was ready when the trumpet blew. The sound of that trumpet blowing three blasts sent us into momentary Pandemonium. We had to line up, youngest in front, and march in very orderly fashion out into the Hall. It took three minutes to get order!

Suzanne opened the door, and we followed behind, pushing and hurrying. Once in the Hall, though, our line slowed. The first time you saw the Christmas tree it simply took your breath, and you had to stand frozen in place just looking.

There was a giant fifteen-foot cedar reaching way above the rail of the balcony with real candles flickering here and there on its branches. The crackling, merry fire in the huge fireplace made dancing sparkles in silver icicles and many-colored balls. The smell of burning cedar twigs thrown in the fire was part of it, too. And under the tree—under the tree were so many packages of all shapes and sorts that they spilled out into the room. Some smaller ones were stuck up among the tree branches. There were even packages between the arches along the balcony which only Daddy and John could reach without going up the stairs.

Daddy began calling our names as he picked up packages carefully labeled with three-inch initials so he, with his poor eyesight, could easily read them. When he called your name, it was so terribly exciting, you thought you couldn't stand it. It seemed your heart had gotten even into your fingers and your feet.

"Charles Cogswell! This looks suspicious. Be careful, it might bite!"

"Suzanne Wynston, come and get it!"

"James Stanley, here are the poker and ashes you've been waiting for."

"Brenda Victoria, rats flee before ya, what could this thing be in this big box?" (That big red package that had been on top of the wardrobe for a month was for *me*!)

"Ginny the Ripper, come to my slipper, maybe this is just what you wanted."

Packages seemed to be flying everywhere, and I was so busy opening mine in a spot I'd chosen over by the bookcase, I forgot to watch the boys when they got their handkerchiefs. I was examining a doll's sewing machine with great pride when Charles sidled up holding a new air rifle.

"Look what I got!" he bragged. "Boy, I wish it weren't already dark so I could try it out now."

"And see what I have!" I exclaimed, running my finger over my little red machine. "It will really sew!"

"Yeah," he responded, still looking at his gun. And then to my dismay he pulled a handkerchief out of his pocket and wiped a

speck of dust from the barrel of his gun. There could be no mistaking those big loopy hemming stitches. It was the handkerchief I'd made for him.

"Oh, thanks for the hanky," he said as an afterthought as he walked off.

I went over to see how Mamma was doing. She had a box of rich pine splinters from Stanley and Charles and a bulb planted in a little pot of stones Jackie had helped Suzanne and me put together. She smiled and hugged me as she offered me one of her chocolate covered cherries Brantley had sent from Canada.

"Did you see how Charles liked his handkerchief?" she asked, pushing my hair behind my ears.

"He's using it for a polishing rag," I said.

"But he has to use it that way," she said. "That's the way boys are made. And it's so nice to have a brand-new handkerchief to polish a brand-new gun."

Suzanne came running to hug Mamma then. "My doll!" she squealed. "Look at my doll! She drinks and wets! And see all her clothes, a *whole* box full!"

It was time for the orange rolling. Daddy opened a bag of oranges and rolled them from the tree towards the other end of the Hall. Everyone went running to catch one. After that you could smell orange peel burning mixed with the melted wax smell, and the smell of hard candy. Pat peeled an orange for me, never mentioning her earlier threat.

As we sang Christmas carols and listened to the Christmas story, I hugged my knees up under my chin casting occasional glances toward my sewing machine, book, and new sweater. I knew that Christmas was the most beautiful and happiest time of all.

Orman and Brantley were almost never home for Christmas that I can remember because they were so far away in school and involved in church work. We had an early Christmas about the first of December getting their packages in the mail. Mamma made them each a batch of fudge, and Charles said he guessed he'd have to leave home before he ever got his own batch of fudge. A shirt, socks, a tie, maybe a new belt would complete the package. I dreaded growing up and receiving only such boring things as those.

But one Christmas was very, very special because Orman did come home, and it was the first time we saw our first nephew. He was born to Orman and Margaret on September 2, 1949, but

Christmas was the first time they could make the long trip from seminary in New Orleans. It was a long wait to see little Thomas Orman Knight.

Jackie marvelled at being an aunt. She was the one who had gotten the mail the day the announcement arrived. When she ran in the door saying breathlessly over and over, "It's come! It's come!" someone had to hold her down to get the letter and find out what had come. Once or twice I sneaked up on her when she was brushing her hair in front of the mirror, and I heard her saying to herself in wonderment, "I'm an aunt, I'm really an aunt."

I was just seven and Suzanne was three. They said we were aunts, too. But that was a little hard to understand. If we weren't old enough to be mothers, how could we be old enough to be aunts? Aunts were always older than mothers; ours were.

As Christmas drew near and Orman wrote to say exactly when he would arrive, we began counting the days and finally the hours. Just after Charles had figured out it would be 168 hours, he told me that since the baby was a boy I wouldn't be able to watch him get his bath. I said that I could, and we were launched into a gigantic fuss that turned into a fight, during which I committed the terrible misdemeanor of kicking. I was severely scolded and sent outdoors to get over being mad.

Orman was always punctual. If he said he would arrive at seven o'clock in the evening, he was almost always there by seven o'clock or maybe a little earlier. And I guess he was on time that day before Christmas Eve, too. But still it seemed he would never come.

Stanley was first to see the car lights. We ran down the stairs, Stanley and Charles sliding down the banister like two streaks of arm and leg lightning. Somehow, though, as fast as we were coming down, Jackie was the one who threw the door open and grabbed the fuzzy bundle out of Orman's arms. The bundle began to cry as it was opened up. We all crowded around to peer in at the tiny hands and little screwed up face.

Tommy was getting quiet again in Orman's arms as he said, "Now, now, son," when Daddy burst out laughing and the rafters resounded with the jollity of it.

"Imagine!" Daddy burst out. "My son saying 'my son'!" He laughed again uproariously, and Tommy started crying again.

Mamma led Margaret with the baby upstairs to help her get him to sleep in the cradle all prepared for the occasion. Jackie got out the Japanese fruitcake. Orman said, "Wow! Mom knew just

what I'd want, didn't she?"

Suzanne loved dolls; she would have loved a thousand if she had had them. It was hard for her to understand that Tommy was not a doll and that she could have just one turn at holding him while sitting in the middle of the bed. I was a little afraid he might break when I held him, but Suzanne was confident as she held him tightly and cooed like a real little mother.

I enjoyed watching the baby's bath more than holding him. Contrary to Charles's prophesy, I did see his bath. Maybe I wasn't supposed to, but I did. Margaret was giving Tommy his bath near the heater in the east room and I just walked in and watched as she so carefully washed ears and all, taking time along to tease a smile from her beautiful baby. There was a warmth and joy between mother and son that made me feel so good. When she finished bathing him, she let me put good smelling powder on him. Then I rushed outside to tell Charles all about it.

That Christmas it snowed. Stanley got a plastic flute among his gifts. When he played it outside so he wouldn't wake the baby, there was a sharp clear echo from the next white hill. The hemlock trees would now and then shrug their shoulders and send little puffs of snow scattering to the ground. The woodpile looked like a funny kind of house buried in the snow.

We had a snowball fight. "One of these days Tommy will be big enough to play," yelled Charles to me, "and he'll show you that girls can't ever win."

I was trying to think of something smart to yell back at him when a snowball hit me smack in the mouth. I jumped behind a nandina bush to make myself a snowball, and from then on the war was on. It was funny how hot you could get under your coat and yet how frozen your fingers would be even inside mittens.

As we thawed our fingers by the kitchen stove, Mamma made hot chocolate with marshmallows in it and the big girls passed filled cups around along with cookies and cake.

It was a happy Christmas, little Tommy's first. Mamma had knitted him a blue cap, and she said he looked like Orman's baby pictures wearing it. Daddy laughed at her and said she knew Tommy was too little to look like anybody yet. Mamma said that he was pretty as a picture, anyway. And Charles said disdainfully, "Mamma, boys aren't *pretty!*"

Whether he was pretty or looked like his daddy or whatever, there was no doubt that everyone was very proud of Tommy.

እ⍲ ⍲ ⍲

Winter brought chilly winds, cold chores, ice castles along red clay banks by the trail to the cabin schoolhouse, the reading of Charles Dickens in the evenings, and popcorn. Winter also brought sickness with ice and snow. But in the dead of winter, jonquils began to bloom, and sunsets were some of the prettiest. Winter came just before spring every year.

Ginger wrote home from Rabun Gap that she was going on a field trip with her sociology class. They would travel to Milledgeville and have a guided tour of Georgia's mental hospital. "We'll pass right by Pinedale," she wrote. "Jackie, you and the kids come out about ten-thirty a.m. on February 5 and wave to me."

That day turned out to be a very cold one, especially in the morning. If you found a place that the wind hadn't found yet, where there was a blanket of sunshine, you could get warm around the edges. You could turn yourself like browning a piece of toast in the oven. But Ginger had said wait for her opposite the mailbox. Frost was still on the ground there, and the wind was playing with our coat flaps and laughing at us for forgetting our mittens. Stanley said we might as well be warm while we waited and that he knew a good spot.

There was a beautiful place of sunshine in the corn patch, and it was in full view of the road, too. We would be able to see Ginger and wave without our teeth chattering. We clustered amongst the dried, brown corn stalks with our backs to the sun and waited again.

We sang a song or two, counted cars, and played "Guess the Make of the Car," at which Charles and Stanley were professionals, if you can be a professional "Guess the Make of the Car" player! They could tell by the sound of the motor when a car topped the hill at Fairplay Road whether the car was a Ford, Chevrolet, or what! I couldn't even tell after it came over the next hill and rounded the curve coming into full view.

But I did recognize the deep drone of the schoolbus coming. We all began to jump up and down, our hands ready to wave. As the bus came around the curve we shouted, "Hi, Ginger! Hi!" "Hey, Ginger, look! Look here!" "GIN-ger! LOOK!"

Everyone on the bus looked at us in astonishment, everyone except Ginger. We could see her, but her head was bent, and she was busily doing something with her hands. The bus disap-

peared, and we froze into statues of disappointment, finally remembering to close our mouths so we wouldn't swallow so
much cold air.

"She was writing us a note," said Jackie dismally. "We were in
the wrong place, and now she thinks we just didn't come."

"Well," said Stanley practically, "if she wrote us a note, then
she must have dropped it where she expected us to be. Let's go
see."

Sure enough there was a tightly rolled ball of paper in the
driveway opposite the mailbox. We crowded around while
Jackie read it.

"Hi!" the note said in hurried bumpy letters. "Wish you all
could go with me to Milledgeville. But they could probably do
without that many 'nuts'! Y'all be good. I love you even if you
are a bunch of nuts. Ginger."

"If only she knew that we did come," said Jackie looking wistfully up the hill where the bus had disappeared. "Well, you can
tell her when you write to her," said Stanley. "In the meantime,
let's go get warm. I'll beat you to the house."

The next time Ginger came home, she brought us each a candy
bar in addition to the little individual packs of cereal she'd saved
from her breakfast trays. "Because you got so cold for nothing,"
she said. "The girl behind me told me to look at the funny sight
out the window, but I was busy writing the note and ignored
her."

The dreariness of winter did come. It always came sometime
after the excitement of Christmas and of the New Year were all
over. The year of the Big Illness the dreariness came sometime in
February. It seemed that the oaks had been bare forever and that
we would never again be able to go out without our coats and
scarves. The warm spell that usually came in January had come
and gone. We had had an exciting snow in early February deep
enough to make a little snowman, although he had trash sticking
out of him. But all that was past now. It was just plain cold, and
lessons were tedious.

I had started English grammar under Daddy's guidance that
year, and I wasn't real sure it was as much fun growing up as I'd
sometimes thought it would be. Words were so exciting in books
where they made you see things happening. And it was so much
fun to put them together on a blank piece of paper and make it
come to life. What did it matter whether you knew the difference

between adverbs and adjectives or even that there were such things? I rebelled inside as I took a sentence apart. It was much nicer simply to read it.

I knocked at Daddy's study door one day, and he called, "Who is it?"

"It's me," I answered, wanting to go in and warm my feet by his fire.

He opened the door and looked down at me, not really sternly. "How would it have sounded if Jesus had said as he walked on the water, 'It's me, Peter, don't be afeared'? Oh, come in and warm up, lassie."

It didn't take me long to warm up. Holding each foot up to the fire momentarily, I seethed inside with raw rebellion. As I started out Daddy held the door for me as if I were a lady and said, "Language is the clothing for your thoughts, my dear. A thought surely deserves to be dressed in its very best when it enters into the world."

"Yes, sir," I said and went outdoors to get cold again.

Sitting on the highest of the Council Rocks on Pine Hill (so named by Mamma who imagined Indians having meetings there) with my coat pulled close around my legs, I tasted the winter day, the ice-blue, pine-needles, brown-leaf day. What was bothering me was that Daddy was right—and I didn't want him to be right. If I had to do the grammar, somehow it would be better if I could feel justified in hating it. "Who cares anyway?" I thought out loud and inside the answer came, "You care, I care, the best is all that I'll settle for." But the rebellion was still there as I walked back towards the house saying "ain't" to each bush I passed, just for spite.

Just when things are looking gloomy, something really bad happens. Suzanne and I came in one afternoon to find the house unusually quiet. Jackie hushed us at the door. As we warmed our hands by the kitchen stove, she explained that Daddy was very sick with the flu.

"What's the flu?" I asked, remembering the word only in connection with the chimney.

"Well, it's a real, real bad cold," Jackie explained.

"Oh, that's not so bad then," Suzanne said. "I've got a bad cold, too."

"Well, maybe he'll be too sick to teach about verbs and things for a day or two anyway," I said playing with the griddle holder, hating what I had said as soon as it was out.

"Brenda! You should be ashamed!" Jackie scolded, and then she sat down suddenly on top of the woodbox with her hand to her forehead.

Mamma came in and, seeing Jackie white and shaking, began to feel her cheeks. "You go to bed," she said. "I'll wrap up an iron to keep your feet warm."

"But, Mamma, you need me to cook..."

"We'll manage," Mamma said, already wrapping the iron in a heavy towel. It smelled scorchy like ironing day. "When you're sick, you're sick. Here, take this and go to bed. I'll be up to see about you in a little."

Jackie looked miserable as she left the kitchen to creep up the stairs. I watched her shadow pass the translucent window and then a gloom crept in. The winter sunshine outside was fading fast, and the wind was rattling the kitchen window and making the great tall pines outside moan and groan. It was the same sound that was happy if you were happy, too.

Mamma went back in the study where Daddy had gone to bed. While she was gone I got an ear of dry corn out of the store-room and began parching kernels of it on top of the stove. They didn't taste very good, but it was fun to watch them dance as they got hot.

The next day Stanley got sick, then Charles, and even Suzanne. Jackie was so sick that she could barely even drink broth, but Stanley didn't have it quite as bad. That's why he got over it so much quicker, I guess. After a couple of days he felt like teasing me when I took him a glass of water. "How about holding a book up for me to read so I won't have to get my arms out in the cold," he said, and then laughed at me when he saw that I really would do it.

But just when Stanley got to feeling better and came dragging down the stairs, the final blow came. As if she had waited until someone responsible was well enough to take over, Mamma got very, very pale and her cheeks sagged. Quietly she went to bed and when I tiptoed into her room, all I could see was the very top of her brown head.

Daddy was still no better. Stanley had to walk to town the second time to get Dr. Garrison who looked very serious, I thought, as he walked out of the big west doors with his black bag, talking to Stanley as he went. I thought I simply could not bear what was happening. "Well, maybe he'll be too sick to teach for a day or two," I'd said when I first heard Daddy was sick. How *could* I have said that? Even though it was wet now after a cold rain, I went out to the big oak tree behind the hemlocks and, huddled in my old black coat that used to be Jackie's, I cried uncontrollably. "God, I'm really sorry," I sobbed as I clenched my fists in my pockets. "I'm so sorry. I didn't mean it. Do you know that?"

I didn't hear Stanley coming. All of a sudden he was there, and he wasn't laughing at me for crying. For once he wasn't laughing at me. He just put his long arms around me and held me for a minute without saying anything.

"They're going to be okay," he said then. "They're all going to be all right. The doctor left some stronger medicine for Dad, and he's asleep now. He's going to be okay, I tell you."

"But," I said trying to talk without crying, "it's all my fault everybody's sick." Then I told him what I had said and how I had felt when Daddy first got sick.

He did laugh then. Loud, so loud that it echoed from the wet trees and drifted down through the woods.

"Do you think God is so little that he would punish everybody for one little sentence you said? God just doesn't operate that way. All you need to worry about is getting in that house and getting warm before you get sick, too."

Stanley got tired of fixing broth and toast and cornmeal mush with lumps in it. He decided a cake would be a nice change and enlisted my help in remembering how to make one. We decided on a chocolate loaf cake. That should be easy enough. For the first time in days things were really interesting. I was even glad I wasn't sick, something I hadn't been sure about before.

We got flour all over the kitchen and used almost every spoon and cup. We took turns stirring the nice dark brown batter, though Stanley's turns were the ones that made it turn smooth and shiny. It smelled delicious while cooking. I was sure everyone would realize they weren't sick anymore when they smelled it, but there were no footsteps on the stairs, not even Suzanne's.

The cake looked good when we took it out, just not quite as puffy as Jackie's always did. But it was hard to bite. It was so hard it made my teeth ache. Just the same it was good, and I proudly carried some to all the patients. They tried real hard to seem impressed, but Jackie was the only one who succeeded. She acted as if Stanley had worked a small miracle.

The real miracle came a few days later when finally one by one the family began to gather in the kitchen again. It was wonderful to have even one bed made up and all smoothed out upstairs. It was nice when Daddy felt like teaching again, too, and I vowed to myself to try very hard to do my best. It was a long time before Mamma felt like singing while she worked or before Suzanne stopped coughing, but at least no one had to stay in bed anymore. And it was good to go to bed at night without being choked by the smell of vapor rub.

The March wind howling around the house, blowing smoke back down the chimneys, didn't sound so threatening with everyone together again. It even made it cozy and warm inside. The oak trees were still bare, but their shadows lay across the ground longer every day. While winter was growing old, spring was getting ready to be born.

Chapter Seven
Mystery Unveiled

Single seasons don't begin to hold all of life. Many times things that happen spill from one season into another. Certainly revelations of growing up don't fit into neat capsules of time, but sprangle along like wet-weather branches seeking a true stream bed. The tiny streams of wonderment start even before you realize that there's more to growing up than reaching a certain penciled mark on the kitchen door.

Learning about babies was one of those sprangly processes. The beginning of it, I guess, was when Suzanne was born. But being only three, I didn't wonder much, but just accepted the fact that wherever she had come from she was there. After all, Pat said that those tiny silver spider webs strung from grass to grass early in the morning were fairies' blankets hung out to dry. I never saw the fairies, but every dewy morning their blankets appeared to prove they'd been sleeping on our lawn again. Magic was easy to believe.

Some little springs enter the brook from underground so insignificantly that only if you bend down close do you see a tiny ripple on the sandy bottom, just enough to keep the minnows excited. Others enter with a gush, and you can pin an oak leaf together in the shape of a cone to get a delicious drink as from a fountain.

Learning about babies came both ways—little insignificant ideas formed, overheard sentences paused in midair, questions that nagged me for an answer, and finally a gush of understanding. It came when I was grown up enough, not in height, but in depth.

"No, you're all the baby I need from now on," Mamma told Suzanne who had asked if we couldn't have another baby.

"But I don't want to be the baby always. I'm getting too big to be the baby now, Mamma."

"Well, it has to stop somewhere, Honey. So just run and play now."

"Oh, Mamma, please..."

"Scoot now."

So that mission had failed. Suzanne came up the corridor where I had stood listening. "It's no use," she whispered, and the spring on the back door whined as we went out.

Jackie was sitting on the stone under the north dogwood cutting up some apples for a supper pie.

"What are you two looking so gloomy about?" she asked, tossing an apple core to a brown hen who suddenly had several feathered friends.

"It's just not fair," said Suzanne, tossing her brown braids. "Being the baby, I mean."

"Oh, that. Are you still worrying about that? Listen, I would love to have been the baby. Look at me. I'm right in the middle. I'm not in the oldest half of the family, and I'm not one of the youngest ones, either. How do you think I feel? You make such a to-do over Pat and Ginger when they come home, practically worshiping the ground they walk on, and they make a to-do over you because you're little and cute. Yes, I think it would be fun to be the youngest."

It was always when Jackie was vehement that I noticed the scar on her forehead where she'd been stung by a guinea wasp. It was a perfectly round little hole. Now I dropped my eyes and screwed my feet in the dust. "We like you, too," I mumbled. "It's just that you're always here...you know."

"I know."

"Anyway," said Suzanne bringing us back to the subject at hand, "I wish we could get a baby. I wonder why we can't get just one. How did Mamma and Daddy get us?"

Jackie sat with the knife poised in a stunned midair position. She looked as if she'd just been asked to make a speech at the White House which to Jackie would be disastrous. I was hoping she would answer. I was too big to ask such a question myself, but I sure did want to know the answer to it.

The knife finally came down and sliced through the apple, laying it open in two neat heart-shaped halves. Jackie fingered a brown seed and then put it in her mouth. "You ask too many questions," she said around it. "Run play."

It was a few weeks after that when Stanley was given a morning off from lessons to "take Scamp off," whatever that meant.

"It's time to take Scamp off," Daddy said at breakfast. "I talked with Mr. Loggans last week, and we made arrangements."

"Will you be back by dinner?" Mamma asked Stan.

"Oh, I'll just eat when I get here. The last time I took that cow off, she gave me an awful time. She wanted to graze everybody's pasture along the way and then when we got to the right one, she didn't want to go through the gate."

"Well, now, you just take your time, son," said Daddy. "This one's going to make fine stock for us, I think, and it's quite worth the extra mile you'll have to go."

Suzanne and I finished our breakfast before Stan did, and we ran to the stable. We climbed up the rough board ladder into the loft and lay in the hay waiting.

"What's he taking her for?" Suzanne whispered.

"Oh, you know," I said, not knowing at all. There was something very mysterious about it all.

"Is he going to leave her there?" she asked anxiously.

"Probably. Well, maybe."

We could hear Scamp scraping the bottom of the feed trough with her tongue, getting the last grains of corn. It made me have chills up and down my spine to hear her rough tongue on the boards. It was like listening to Suzanne scrape her nails down a concrete wall just to make me squirm.

Stanley and Charles came, jumping over the pasture wall with a thump rather that going through the bars. Through a crack we watched them put the rope on Scamp who stood docilely swishing her tail and chewing.

"I wish they'd let me go," Charles said resentfully.

"I do, too. We'd explore down the river a little on the way home. Maybe next year."

"Maybe when you go back for her. How about that?"

"Yeah. I guess. But I doubt if he'll let you really. Unless I were to have trouble with her."

"Well...?"

"We'll see," said Stan as he led Scamp out the door.

Bulb transplanting time came. As we reset bulbs along the driveway at the foot of the hill, sometimes we ran and warmed our hands momentarily in the spring, the magically warm spring. Charles explained that the spring water was always the same temperature, but that in summer when the air was so hot the water felt very cold and in winter when the air was cold the water felt warm. It really felt good to hold your hands in the spring a minute, then dry them quickly on a wool scarf.

Christmas passed and in January, during a warm spell, the jasmine put out little yellow blooms which were killed back by a heavy frost. We skated down Sunny Lawn on our way to the cabin, our eyes dazzled by a million frost-jewels set on fire by the sun.

Day after day, morning and night, Scamp was milked and the bucket hung over the flour bin on a hook until someone strained the milk. Scamp didn't seem to have changed any at all that I could tell. She still looked the same and smelled the same and still chewed her cud the same, looking, as Daddy said, like a woman chewing gum.

February passed into March, and the winds howled and moaned in the pine trees. "I think it sounds as it must sound on the rocky coast of Maine," Daddy told Mamma. Something about the way he said it made me think of the old saying he'd laughingly referred to several times, that if a person had a space between his teeth, he'd cross the seas some day. He did have such a nice space between his teeth. I wished mine were like that.

It was near the end of March or the first of April when Daddy heard the radio announcement that sent the whole household into high excitement. He was listening to the "news on the hour" and was turning it off when the special bulletin came in. There was a small two-year-old boy found in the Cornelia bus station with a note pinned to his shirt. The note said, "Please take care of him. I can't." All he had with him was a little brown bag with one change of clothes. The bulletin said if anyone were interested in giving the boy a foster home, they should contact the local welfare office immediately.

"What's a foster home?" Suzanne asked.

"It's a temporary home for children who have no parents," explained Daddy.

"Children stay in foster homes until someone wants to adopt them and have them for keeps," said Mamma.

"Like an orphanage?" I asked.

"Not exactly. It's more like a real home for them."

"Why didn't his mother want him?"

"Oh, she wanted him," said Jackie with a look of tears about to come. "She just couldn't keep him."

"You children run along now," said Daddy. "I want to discuss this with your mother."

Discuss it? Did that mean that maybe...? We went to tell the boys about it, and Charles actually stood on his head because he was so pleased it was a boy. We all came back in to see how the discussion was going. The boys went up to the Little Room to listen and left us the keyhole.

"How could we let him go to someone else after we fell in love with him?" Mamma asked. I could tell with my turn at the keyhole that she was in her straw rocking chair with her hands in her lap.

"But maybe no one else would ever want him," said Jackie softly, and we realized that she had been called into the discussion.

"He does have to stay somewhere. And we could give him a good home here. But, Eula, if you think it best not to pursue, we certainly will not. It's really up to you."

There was a silence in which I could hear the fire popping and a wet log stewing. Suzanne let me look again. Mamma's hands were in a knot now. Was it going to be yes? Oh, please, let it be yes! I pictured a little blonde boy waiting just for us to call. Then I knew, just as Suzanne pushed me aside for her turn, what Mamma's answer would be. I had seen her hands relax and her fingers meticulously smoothing out the balled up handkerchief.

"There's always room under a mother hen's wing for one more little biddy," she said.

"Oh, goody, goody, goody!" Jackie cried and the door burst open before we had time to escape. Daddy laughed, being in one of his festive moods.

"I can tell this little boy is going to be blessed with a number of mothers," he said.

Immediately Stanley was sent to warm up the Packard which hadn't been driven in days. Stanley had his learner's license and was allowed to drive on special occasions. This was certainly a special occasion. But the car would not crank. A kettle of water was put on to heat. Hot water poured in the radiator always helped. But this time, even with kettle after kettle of water until the stove's reservoir was nearly empty, the motor wouldn't turn over. It was pushing time. With the whole family behind or beside her, the Packard couldn't help herself and the whine of the starter finally changed to the loud, if uneven, roar of the motor as the car started down the north driveway. Stanley jumped quickly into the open door where he had been pushing. He applied the brakes while Daddy and Mamma got in the other side. Mamma remembered to wave back to us as they bumped down the road and Stanley tooted the horn as a note of triumphal exit.

Then the waiting began. Eternal waiting. Jackie sent Suzanne and me to see if the crocuses were up as an excuse to get us out of her way for a little while.

The crocuses were up, but not in bloom. Mamma watched for them carefully each year because they were in a little corner of lawn between the birdbath and a holly where she would never accidentally see them. It was a little bay of lawn with bushes on three sides. The birdbath was a great stone with a very nice dip in its flat side where we kept water if there wasn't enough rain. Or sometimes Mamma put whey in the dip after she made cottage cheese. The birds for some reason enjoyed that awful stuff. Anyway, you couldn't see the crocus bed without going around the birdbath, with its background of nandina bushes, and entering the bay. Even then you had to get down and look closely to find the tiny crocus blades. But if they were in bloom, their little purple cups traced with orange looking up bravely from the grass, you'd see them immediately. It was a special day when they bloomed.

But this day was special without the crocuses. Suzanne and I held hands and "wrung the dish towel" in pure excitement. The little practice in gymnastics gave Crusoe a reason to bark, and he ran along beside us yipping at our heels as we jumped off the pasture wall and ran down Sunny Lawn. Scamp was grazing on Sand Flat and raised her head in slow surprise, grass sticking out of the side of her mouth, as we came to a breathless stop near her.

"Boy, Scamp, you sure are getting big," Suzanne said to her, rubbing her broad side. "What's making her so fat?"

"Sure isn't all this grass," I thought out loud. A memory flashed through my mind of Stan leading her off that morning last fall. He and Charles went back to get her later, but they wouldn't tell me anything about it. Except Stan said, "We didn't even know when Suzanne was going to be born. But...you'll find out someday."

I looked at Scamp all bulged out chewing peacefully on crisp spring grass. Putting my ear to her stomach, I listened just out of curiosity.

"What are you *doing*?" Suzanne wanted to know.

"Just listening to her dinner digesting," I said, and it was the truth. "Race you back to the house!"

We sang the Packard home while Jackie cooked supper. "Packard, oh, Packard, bring Mamma and Daddy and Stanley and Someone back ho-o-me." Pat had made up that little adaptable song when she was part of the waiting ones.

Jackie warned us that the little boy just might not be in the Packard when it came, but we really didn't listen.

Charles heard the first rumble of the car way down in the lane. We stood on the front steps and watched the lights creeping up the hill. Suzanne and I argued about which of us would hold the baby first. Jackie said we were both too little, and Charles said he wouldn't need holding anyway because he was a little boy, not a baby.

Then Mamma and Daddy were getting out of the car and Stanley drove around to park in the garage. Mamma only had her same black leather purse in her hand. Daddy's hands were hanging free. There was no little boy. With an aching gulp I turned to run into the lamplit house, pausing inside the door to hear the answer to Suzanne's question—"When are we going to get him?"

"We're not, Honey," Mamma said in a voice full of gentleness, but finality.

"We were a little too late. Someone else had already gotten him," said Daddy. "No, Suzy-que, don't cry..."

Scamp always came to the stable and stood at the wall waiting for feed time. She might wander in the meadow all day eating luscious sweet grass, drinking at the brook, and taking midday rests under the persimmon trees. Or she might graze on Tulip Hill or Lespedeza Patch. But she would always come home at night. She sometimes even stayed up in the Firewood Heights woods in the daytime and had gone as far as Orchard Corner where the fence stopped her. But as the sun slanted long fingers through the trees, Scamp would come plodding home.

But on that day in late May Scamp did not come home. Daddy had let Stan and Charles go to a concert at Piedmont College in Demorest. Stanley had had his sixteenth birthday and now had his driver's license. Since Scamp's milk was dried up now, Suzanne and I should be able to handle her, Daddy had said, so the boys had left her with us.

We would have been able to take care of her if she had been

there. But she didn't come no matter how much we called, "Soo, cow, soo, cow."

"You don't say it right," said Suzanne, "You've got to let it come out slow and long. That's what she's used to."

"Well, you call her then. I'll spread the leaves out in her stall."

We had gathered two burlap bags full of fresh dry leaves from the woods. Now I wondered if we shouldn't have been looking for her instead of raking leaves. I looked at the nice bed they made, crunchy-soft. Any cow would feel blessed to sleep here in this nice place. After all, cows wouldn't be afraid of the dark corner behind the door. I stepped quickly out into the twilight to scan the pasture for any sign of Scamp.

"Listen," said Suzanne holding up one hand, "I thought I heard her bell."

But if it had been her bell, it didn't ring again. Stars were beginning to come out, and I rubbed my arms to warm them.

"Any luck, girls?" called Mamma.

"She's too far away to hear us," I answered.

"Or just not answering," Mamma said coming towards the wall. "Here's a flashlight. Don't go far, but just look down around Tulip Brook and around the edges of the pasture. She might be behind a tree or something."

"Why wouldn't she come when she heard us call?"

"Well, she might be sick. And anyway she can be very stubborn. I left some bread in the oven and I'll have to go check on it. Jackie will be out to help you in a jiffy. She and Daddy are walking the fences to the north to be sure Scamp didn't get out toward the highway."

Suzanne wanted to hold the flashlight, but I explained that the oldest always carried the light. The light made a little pool for us as we walked into the edges of the woods up by Lespedeza Patch. Every twig that broke under our feet sounded like a pistol crack. Every tree seemed to hide something monstrous behind it, the very same trees that were so sane and loving in the daytime.

In the ravine between Lespedeza Patch and Tulip Hill there were perfect places for a cow to hide if she wanted to. We had hidden there many times ourselves in hide-and-go-seek games. There were potholes where floods had rounded out the red clay just as a potter might. There were little caves under the overhang of banks. Crab apple trees touched limbs in a rough caress. Underbrush grabbed at our dresses and at our skin as we looked into our favorite spots which were ominous in the blackness.

There was no Scamp, no scent of fresh manure and dew-dampened cow hair, no sound of rhythmic munching.

"It's a good thing she's not there," I said as we backed out from under a low crab apple limb.

"Why?"

"Because she might have broken her leg getting down in that ditch."

"But she goes there a lot. 'Specially when it's hot."

"Yes. But this might have been one time too many. She is getting older, you know, not as good at scrambling maybe. She might have broken her leg like Old Red."

The grass was wet and squeaky under our feet. We went up Tulip Hill shining the light into the thickets on either side, hoping anytime to see the fat brown sides of Scamp and to hear her apologetic "moo." The boys often milked Scamp on top of Tulip Hill in the summertime so we thought maybe she was ready for that. But she wasn't there.

"What happened to Old Red when she broke her leg?" Suzanne asked fearfully.

"They had to shoot her. They had her butchered and ate her. We probably helped to eat her; we just didn't know what it was. You know a cow's no good with a broken leg."

"Oh, how awful! Scamp just can't..."

"Sssh! What was that?"

It was a screech owl. It must have been on top of the tree house in the oak tree. It sounded that close, but we couldn't see it with the flashlight. The hairs on my arms were standing straight out. Then we saw the bobbing light at the top of Sunny Lawn and heard Jackie's cheerful, "Yoo-hoo!"

"You haven't seen anything of her?" she asked as she caught up with us.

"Not a thing. I guess the meadow's next."

"Well, let's go. We've *got* to find her. The boys already think we can't get along without them..."

"Do you think she's sick?" Suzanne asked.

"Well, probably not sick, but..."

"But what?"

"Let's just go find her."

Along the brook there were nice sandy beaches where Scamp had made regular visits leaving water-filled tracks and dark cow piles. The meadow was a beautiful place in daytime with its meandering brook, its willows and beeches, its buttercup and for-

get-me-not grass flats, and our one mulberry tree, the mulberry tree that seemed to be part of a fairy tale. But at night, with creepy things sliding into the water and every bush an unknown, it was not so pleasant. I stepped on a thorn and had to hop the rest of the way because we couldn't see to get it out.

"Soo-cow, S-oo-oo-cow, come on, old Scamp girl. Come to supper."

Jackie stopped then, turned out her light, and told me to do the same. "Listen real, real hard," she whispered.

There was a wind sighing in the tops of the trees. Insects were singing like a see-saw, up and down, up and down.

"Come this way," Jackie whispered, leading us under a persimmon tree and across open grass to a huddle of dark bushes.

Then I heard it. A funny licking sound and a soft little cow sound, not a whole "moo," maybe half of one. Shining her light, Jackie squealed with delight.

"Oh, look, just look!" she cried, going down on her knees.

I stood there amazed watching Scamp licking a little wobbly-legged calf with greasy looking fur. So *that* was what it was all about, all that "taking Scamp off" and her getting fat and everything. It was obvious where that little calf had come from even in the dim, shaky light, for Scamp was definitely not fat anymore.

"Look, she's already learned how to get her supper. Watch her! Isn't she adorable!" Jackie exclaimed. "She's a miracle, that's what she is. One of God's miracles. Oh, Scamp girl, you did a good job!"

"You mean she's a she?" Suzanne asked, attempting to put her arms around the little wet thing, but getting nudged persistently away by Scamp.

"Yes. It's a heifer. Daddy will be glad about that."

"Well, the boys won't," declared Suzanne. "Remember? They wanted a boy. I really don't care. Just so we got her. Now we have a baby after all!"

I ran my hand over Scamp's nose before we left, and she flicked her right ear. "Are you sure she'll be okay there?" I asked.

"Oh, she's fine now. It's warm enough down here for her. But we had to be sure she was okay, and the little calf, too. We'll check on her again tomorrow."

As we walked back up Sunny Lawn, we could see the warm lights of Stone Gables. When we were almost to the top of the hill, Suzanne burst ahead, eager to tell the news. Jackie held out a hand to help me over the wall as I was still hobbling along with a thorn in my foot.

"Do babies come the same way as heifers?" I asked.

Jackie hesitated just a minute and then said, "Yes, and isn't life just terribly interesting! You know," she continued as I limped beside her feeling gloriously knowledgeable and grown-up suddenly, "if people would only look at the things God does every day, they would know how much he cares for them. Why, he writes little notes to us all the time with trees and flowers and stones and..."

"And little heifers," I supplied.

The flashlight wasn't needed now. We were walking by starlight on very familiar ground. I hopped over a pine root and picked a piece of bark from a tree as I held to it momentarily. Jackie paused in front of me by the heavily scented jasmine bush which in sunlight had shiny little leaves, but was now a big dark glob. I could see the outline of her light-colored dress against it.

"Brenda," she said in a very confidential tone, "I'm so glad God made me to be a woman."

I shivered, not just because the air was chilly, but because I had seen a miracle and had caught a glimpse of destiny.

Chapter Eight

Our Honeymooners

Yes, many events come in seasons—floods in spring, fires in fall, canning in summer, snow in winter—but weddings happen anytime. And for a wedding, the world will almost stop turning. Anything that will make a mother cry, a daddy tremble, and make a lovable sister into an untouchable bride should make the world stop, if only for ten minutes.

Pat was the first to have a wedding at our house. Orman, Brantley, and John were already married, but their weddings were not at Stone Gables. That first wedding at Stone Gables caught the boys green in the art of "fixing" the groom's car. They had the audacity to ask Pat's fiance, David Peck, if they could do something to his car! David later admitted that he was quite disappointed when they didn't just do it without asking and was also disappointed that the artwork was so timid no one could really tell for sure what it said!

Pat's wedding brought on the completion of the bathroom which was exciting enough in itself. Her wedding was in June, and the plumbing was finished in May. We ran the water in the lavatory just to see it run—that is, when we were sure Mamma and Daddy weren't noticing. After carrying buckets of water up the hill for years, Daddy's ears were keen to the slightest wasted trickle!

Mamma baked her first and last wedding cake for Pat. It took three bakings to get one just right since the stove wasn't quite level and the layers kept baking lopsided. Finally she got the stove legs even by sliding chips of wood under them. We ate lopsided cake as if it were bread and were almost sorry the last set of tiers came out so even. Jackie put a little ferny archway on the white-iced top tier and hung yucca blossoms on it for bells.

Mamma put it on the buffet in the Hall, and Daddy said she would be in practice when there was another wedding. But Mamma said from then on wedding cakes would be baked elsewhere, and Daddy, after a quick look at her, didn't argue.

Since I was not quite ten when Pat married, it was hard for me to understand what it all meant. But when Jackie made me understand that Pat would spend all of her holidays from teaching with her husband instead of with us, I decided that I didn't like weddings or husbands. Out beyond the hemlocks behind the house where I thought I was all alone, I burst into tears on June 12, Pat's wedding day. The crunch of tires on wood chips and pine cones was so close when I heard it that I didn't have time to get away before Uncle Pete saw me. (Only at a wedding would a car come all the way to the hemlocks.) Uncle Burns, affectionately called by all of us Uncle Pete, got right out, and before I knew it, I was crying on his shoulder. Then I was laughing because he said he had cried when my mother got married. Uncle Pete—cry?

Ginger was the third girl to get married and the last one for awhile. Jackie had been married the year before, and Daddy looked at my skinny twelve-year-old figure and laughingly said I would be a beautiful bride in about ten years, which sounded like another century to me.

Charles had been taking violin lessons for a year, and Ginger wanted him to play at her wedding. We heard the wedding march all summer long. Somehow it seemed unfair to have the wedding march playing as you plodded up the stairs, your arms full of clean clothes which were breathlessly rescued from a thunder shower. How could you pretend to be a bride at a time like that?

Suzanne and I were proud of being asked to sing a duet. We were too big to be flower girls as we'd been at Pat's wedding, and Jackie was the matron of honor. So what else could we be in a small wedding? It was nice to be asked—but all that practicing! Why sing our song for a solid hour every day? It would only take three minutes for the final performance. We practiced until Daddy was satisfied with our harmony, Charles was almost satisfied with our timing, and Ginger said we sounded beautiful.

It was a beautiful song. Ginger had chosen it because she said it was her prayer: "Saviour, like a Shepherd, lead us; much we need thy tender care." But unfortunately, no one at the wedding except the three of us heard the words, because our voices faded

out in pure fright. Since we were on the upper balcony where we couldn't be seen by the guests, no one even knew we sang. After the ceremony people worried Charles to death hugging him and telling him how they enjoyed the wedding march—and his solo, too! He finally left through the back door without even getting any cake. That shows how badly it affected him. He had planned to eat three or four pieces at least.

The boys had learned how to do things up right by the time Ginger and Del got married. Besides tying cans to the axle of their car, and using a profuse amount of paint they promised Mamma was washable, they hid a six-weeks-old kitten under the seat. Then several carloads of us followed Ginger and Del out the drive and up the road. It was hilarious to see that kitten's silhouette appear between Ginger's and Del's heads as they went flying down the road. They wrote us from Texas that Fluffy had enjoyed their honeymoon very much.

The reason I've waited until now to tell about Jackie's wedding is that hers was the one in which we were most involved. Jackie fell in love and was courted right at Pinedale with our help and hindrance. Pat and Ginger were both away at school and/or jobs when they were courted. But Jackie's love story belonged to us in a way because we were part of it from the beginning to the wedding.

It started on a Saturday night. It was late, and Suzanne and I were supposed to be asleep, but we had been telling each other stories and were still wide awake. Ginger and Jackie were talking about Ginger's sweetheart while Ginger rolled her hair. Ginger, who was home from a summer job for the weekend, was trying to describe how really nice Del was.

"I wish you had a boyfriend, Jackie," she said.

"Oh, I really think I'd like to be an old maid and just always live at Pinedale," Jackie said. "I've thought how I can fix the stable up like a house someday when I need a place of my own. Well, it may sound funny, but I'm almost twenty so I have to think about these things."

"Were you thinking of building a barn for the cows?" asked Ginger laughing. "But, Jackie, you know you don't want to be an old maid. Why, you'd be so lonesome. Why don't you go to college and study to be a teacher or something? You would make such a good one!"

"Being an old maid school teacher would be better than just being an old maid, you mean. Well, I'd sort of like to start a nursery school down in the cottage. But I don't want to go to college. I just don't. Anyway, stop worrying about me, I'm all right. Speaking of Del, is he really going to be a preacher?"

"Yes, isn't that wonderful! He's going to seminary in Texas after he graduates from college. It's so far away, I wish I could go with him."

"Well, maybe you can." Jackie cupped her hands around her face to peer out the window. "I wonder what those boys are doing. They *said* they were going to the studio and go straight to bed, but I know they didn't."

"Hey, look!" said Ginger looking out just then as she pinned a last curler in. "Car lights! Now who could that be?"

"Oh, I bet it's John!" Jackie exclaimed. "Let's go see!"

"Go see! And us in housecoats? I've just finished rolling my hair, too. What if it's not John?"

"Well, who else could it be? We're not expecting anyone else."

"We're not expecting him either, remember. What about that friend of Stan's? Maybe he's early."

"Fred Eastham? Why, no, he's not coming till Monday, and from all Stan's said about how slow he is, it'll probably be Wednesday about midnight when he comes. Come on, Ginger." Jackie wrapped her housecoat closely around her. "Here, we'll just take this lamp instead of hunting up a flashlight."

"Can we go?" Suzanne pleaded.

"Indeed you cannot!" Ginger said. "We'll be back in just a wink. Now you go to sleep!"

We sank back under summer sheets obediently, but as soon as we heard the last stair creak, we jumped from the bed to watch them go down the front vista toward the studio and cottage. They were talking in such loud whispers we could almost understand through the open windows. Then we couldn't hear anything except the throb of insects as the light bobbed along down the hill.

The next day Charles told us what he had seen and heard, and we listened for every tidbit of information about the night before. We'd feigned obedient sleep when the girls finally returned. They seemed to be in the middle of an argument, but wouldn't oblige by raising their voices so we could tell what it was all about. Their voices did rise to a little squeak a time or two and subsided into giggles several times, but we never made any sense out of it all.

Charles said it happened something like this.

When Ginger and Jackie got close to the studio and could hear voices, Ginger drew back, insisting that the visitor was not John and she would not be seen in her nightclothes. Jackie was sure it was John for some reason, so she went on and left Ginger waiting reluctantly behind a bush.

It wasn't until Jackie got right to the open studio door that she could see Fred standing just inside. Charles said she looked sort of witchy, her hair wild from a night breeze, the lamp chimney smoked black throwing its dingy light up on her face, and her bedraggled old housecoat hiding her slim figure.

Jackie was terribly shy, and Charles thought she would turn and run, but she just froze there for a minute as everyone else did. Even Fred didn't say anything—Fred who could make the best of any situation, we were to learn later. Then in a weak little voice and with her cutest crooked smile, Jackie made a welcoming speech ending by asking Stan if there were enough cover on the guest bed. "I can bring another blanket when I come to bring you a snack. I'm sure you're hungry after your trip," she said to Fred as she looked at Stan.

"We have plenty of blankets and things," said Stan. "It's too hot for much cover. And Fred said he has some coo—"

"I would indeed enjoy a snack," interrupted Fred, glancing sidewise at Stan. "Of course it would be a shame for you to have to come back so far."

"Oh, I love to walk at night!" said Jackie brightly. "Mamma and Daddy are already asleep, I think, so be making yourself comfortable, and I'll be back in a minute."

"I'll go get it, Jackie," offered Charles.

"Oh—well, okay, come on then."

Charles said that somehow he didn't feel she appreciated his helping her that time. After all, he could have stayed there and made her come all the way back down. She would almost certainly have had to talk to Fred again, too, with his deep voice coming from down in his barrel chest.

Fred was on his way to Florida, it seemed, and had just asked if he might stop by for a day or two. We thought he would probably go on as soon as he could. Florida was such an exciting place to go; he wouldn't want to be delayed long. At least it was an exciting place judging by the stories Daddy told of the years he lived in a tiny cottage on Cape Canaveral. I could almost taste the guavas he described, and picture Daddy easing backwards from a python he met late one evening. He said he didn't know exactly how long it was, but, stretched from one side of the sandy road to the other, neither its head nor its tail were showing. Daddy had brought three or four six-foot rattlesnake skins home to Georgia, skins of rattlers he'd personally conquered. But we could tell by his story that the python was most awesome of all. We listened as if we had never heard it before as Daddy told Fred the story of his finding the great piece of coral we used now for a seat. Fred was duly fascinated.

In fact, Fred seemed more fascinated by Daddy's stories than he was in getting to Florida. He had been here a couple of days and wasn't even talking about leaving.

Mamma said we could have a wiener roast down by the pond. That meant a trip to town to get wieners. Stanley asked if Fred would drive to town with him to purchase supplies. "Why don't you and Charles stay at home and let me take Jackie?" Fred offered. "She probably knows much more about buying groceries. May I?" he asked turning to Jackie who turned pink as a peony and said yes.

They were laughing when they came back. After Jackie had ordered five pounds of hot dogs at Carey's, she left Fred to pick up the package at the meat counter while she gathered up the buns, potato chips and all. Fred began shaking his head when the butcher set the huge package on the counter. "That can't be ours. You've made a mistake," he said. But Jackie came along smiling and saying, "Yes, that's ours. I *think* that will be enough."

Fred told it on himself and said to Mamma, "I didn't know how much a big family eats." It crossed my mind that it must truly be lonesome to be the only child in a family as Fred had been—even though it would be nice to have your own room.

It was when Fred asked Jackie to go boating on the pond that I remembered what Ginger had said to Jackie as she got on the bus the Sunday before. "Try not to be too shy, Jackie. He really seems very nice."

Jackie was doing a pretty good job, I thought. As she dressed to go boating, I begged to be allowed to go, too. "This is something special," she said fastening a barrette in her hair and then refastening it because it didn't suit her. "You'll have special times too some day when you'll want to be alone with just one person."

"Well, why in the world are you dressing up to go out on the pond? What if you fall in?"

"Don't even suggest such a thing! Now go get a book or something and let me get ready in peace."

Stanley, Charles, Suzanne, and I all watched Jackie's and Fred's flashlight bob down the hill and watched it move around on the pond. It was hard to go to bed with something so very interesting taking place, but Mamma came to tuck Suzanne and me in and said positively no more watching out the window. We lay whispering and giggling for a few minutes, mimicking Fred's Virginia accent by talking about "tom-AH-toes" and the "hoose." Then it was simply too tempting, so we crept to the west windows intending to stay only a few minutes.

Was that laughter and singing? It was beautiful coming from the water that way. Oh, to be grown up and have fun like that! Then there was silence from the boaters, and the light was staying in one place right in the middle of the pond, about the place where you step from mud silt to sandy brook bottom when in swimming. I wondered who had the oars. But then it would be Fred, of course. Jackie wouldn't let him know how good she was at rowing herself, not if she were a real heroine.

The frogs were singing at top chorus, and the moon was beginning to shine making milky white avenues between the pine shadows down through the grove. The west door closed gently, and the boys talked low between themselves as they started down to the studio to go to bed. I could see them go down the west terrace walking with their hands in their pockets. They were about even with the first holly tree down spring vista when Suzanne cried out, and I looked back quickly to the pond. The flashlight was not still anymore, but was waving wildly.

"They must have gotten caught in a whirlpool," said Suzanne fearfully, probably thinking about a terrible scene from Bess Streeter Aldrich's *Song of Years*.

"They couldn't have. There aren't any whirlpools in our pond."

About that time the light went out and Jackie screamed. We looked at each other in the moonlit darkness wondering what we should do. "Stanley and Charles will help them," I said, hearing their footsteps break into a run towards the pond. "I wonder if we should tell Mamma and Daddy."

"I don't know. It might get Jackie in trouble. I wonder why they don't turn the light back on. Maybe because the moon's out now."

"Maybe because Jackie fell in with it and got it wet. And she'll be all wet in that dimity dress. You watch here, and I'll go listen and see if Mamma and Daddy heard anything."

From a quiet almost held-breath silence in the Little Room where I tried very hard not to touch the creaky place in the floor, I listened to the conversation below.

"But he is a mighty fine young Christian gentleman," said Daddy.

"Yes. I know that."

"And his intentions seem good right now."

"I hope they are."

"Well, you'll have to admit, Eula, that I am a pretty good judge of character. Now I can just tell by the set of his chin and the look in his eyes that he is a fine person."

"Yes. But it's not easy to think of losing her."

"Well, not long ago you were wondering if our terribly shy little Jackie would ever find anyone. You women..."

Suzanne called out in a stage whisper that Jackie, Fred, and the boys were coming up the front vista. I began to ease out of my place so I could get to the scene of action without giving myself away. Mamma's chair creaked as she said, "You're pretty particular yourself, you know."

"Oh, yes, I certainly am and if I see anything going amiss, I assure you I'll be the first to put a stop to this. After all, he said he was staying for a couple of days, and it's already been four...What in the dickens is going on...?"

Suzanne and I met at the balcony as the others came in. We couldn't see without going down too far and calling attention to ourselves, so we just listened.

"It just tipped over, Mamma, really it did. I don't know why," Jackie was explaining breathlessly.

"It was all my fault," said Fred seriously. "I asked her to sit beside me, and she lost her balance changing seats."

Mamma said, "Hmmmm."

Charles said, "I think what really happened was that Jackie jumped in the water so Fred would rescue her."

There was a lot of laughter, but Jackie wasn't laughing as she came dashing up the stairs dripping from head to toe. Her white dress stuck to her skin below where Fred's army shirt came to. Her face was fiery red, and she snapped "Hush!" when I said, "I told you not to dress up so."

Fred still didn't say anything about going to Florida, not when I was listening anyway. I wondered if Daddy had asked him about his intentions and if they were what they were supposed

to be. I guessed they were since he was still there. One day he borrowed Jackie's typewriter to fill out a form for the United States Army. He looked at Jackie seriously and said, "It feels as if I'm signing my life away."

"When will you leave?" she asked, studying the back of the typewriter as if there might be something wrong with it.

"In ten days I'm due at Fort Bliss, Texas, where I'll be in officers' training school. Before that I'm going back to see Mother and Dad in Warrenton, Virginia." He took her hand and toyed idly with her fingers before he looked up with those ever-so-soft brown eyes of his. "Mother will think I've fallen in the Everglades if I don't call soon. I think I'll call her tonight. May I tell her about you?"

"I'm—not—sure."

Fred looked so attentive and Jackie so sweet that somehow I felt a terrible urge to giggle. I managed to get through the breakfast room, up the corridor, and out the back door before the giggles overcame me. Charles almost strangled me because I wouldn't tell him what was funny, but it really wasn't funny. I just felt like giggling was all.

Fred told Mamma he was leaving Friday morning, so Thursday we planned a picnic as sort of a farewell, I guess. He had really become one of us, and we weren't looking forward to seeing him go. Then something happened that kept him from going for awhile longer.

The picnic lunch was packed and ready sitting on the stone seat outside the kitchen door. But Stanley and Fred who had gone down the hill an hour ago "just for a minute" were still not back. Daddy wasn't planning to picnic since it was such a bright day, but he was as anxious as anyone to get it started, looking out the door every five minutes to see if the two boys were coming.

"What could be keeping them so long?" asked Jackie. "Don't they have any respect for other people's stomachs? I bet they're sitting under a tree somewhere talking politics."

"Now, now, Jackie," said Mamma smoothing her hair as if she were a little girl like me. "Stop fretting so. They'll be here soon. I'm sure they will."

"Well, it's just not fair that they should keep us waiting so long. Do you realize it's after one o'clock? I'm going to go find them." The little round wasp sting scar blazed red on Jackie's forehead.

"No, Jackie. No, don't do that. Wait. They'll come. In just a minute they'll be here."

But they didn't come and they didn't come, not in two minutes, five minutes, or even ten. Mamma began to get worried, and Daddy was thinking of sending me to see about the boys when we heard their voices on the front steps.

As they walked in Stan was holding solicitously to Fred's arm, and Fred was obviously limping. He managed a short laugh and said, terribly apologetically, "I'm sorry to delay the picnic like this. It really was too bad to make everyone wait so long."

"I guess there won't be a picnic," said Stan helping Fred into a chair. "Fred's been snakebitten."

I tightened my hold on the newel post and remembered full force the feel of a large copperhead sliding out from under my bare foot one dark night. Stanley later killed it and said it hadn't bitten me because it was full of little snakes. Mamma had comforted me that night by saying not a one of all us children had been bitten. But now Fred had.

Behind me Jackie made a strange little sound before dashing up the stairs.

"He's okay," Stan said. "We've been to Dr. Garrison's and he gave him the antivenom stuff. Of course this crazy Fred didn't want to go before he told you where we were going," he said to Mamma.

"Well, my goodness, I'm glad you made him go on," Mamma said, finding her voice which sounded a little shaken.

"Boy, it was a big copperhead. I killed him, though; he won't hurt anyone else." Stan was waxing proud of his rescue now.

Fred looked kind of white, but other than that he seemed to be all right as long as he sat down. We had our picnic around him in the Hall after Mamma had gotten a stool and cushion for his foot. We watched with great interest and some horror as his leg swelled and turned black. He said he'd be careful the next time he stepped over a log. I was sure I would be, too.

Fred didn't go home that Friday morning, but waited until Sunday instead. He sat in one of the rocking chairs in the Hall most of the time. I wondered if he were really in such pain or if he just wanted an excuse for Jackie to nurse him, which she did. She had gotten all over her mad feelings and even read to him and started learning how to play chess. Occasionally she would run and freshen a cold rag for him. Charles and I talked about it and decided Fred was either really brave not to complain any more than he did, or he was really in love with our Jackie. We made a pact to keep a close watch out for a kiss.

Saturday afternoon Fred was able to limp around pretty well, and he proposed that he and the boys cook dinner that night. Mamma was astonished. Her men never worked in the kitchen unless out of dire necessity. The only time I remember Daddy preparing anything to eat was when Mamma was gone somewhere and he wanted to give Suzanne and me some bread and butter. Not finding the butter, he spread lard on the bread, saying that would just have to do. Another time he tried to wash the dishes. I had to go out in the corridor and hide behind the door to smother a laugh. He did look so funny, his legs spread apart, his back bowed, trying to get no more than the tips of his fingers wet. If he had been working in the creek, he wouldn't have minded the water, but dishwater was different.

Anyway, Mamma was astonished, but she agreed to it. Ladies were not allowed in the kitchen after preparations began. Even little ladies were not allowed. The boys drove Suzanne and me away from the crack between the kitchen doors.

Mamma and Jackie didn't know what to do with themselves, being able to sit down at such a busy time of day. Daddy, who was neither a chef nor a lady, brought hints from the kitchen that made us more cautious than ever. Once he asked, "Hasn't that old brown bowl been retired for a dog dish?" If it hadn't been for the twinkle in his eyes behind his glasses, I would have been sure the boys were mixing something in that old cracked bowl.

Jackie ran toward the kitchen door when there was a loud clatter, but she went back to her chair when uproarious laughter spouted from the kitchen. After that there was a lot of scraping and sweeping.

Finally Fred came out and in very fine style, even with a limp, seated us at the table. In a minute Stan came out with a white towel folded over his arm and handed us each a typewritten menu. The menu wasn't one to choose from, but just to let us know what we were having. There was only one meat listed—"rattlesnake meat, fresh today." The salad was called "fresh oak leaves," and the drink was "mountain dew." But when the plates came there was spaghetti and meat sauce, lettuce leaves with tomato slices, toasted bread, and more fresh spring water. They had made instant pudding for dessert, but Charles had spilled it on the floor. So we had bread and jelly instead. We didn't know until later that the spaghetti had been spilled in the sink in the act of draining.

That night after everyone was in bed (we thought), an unmis-
takable male trio struck up a Spanish serenade under the west
windows. Jackie said softly, as we pushed to the windows trying
to see without being seen, "Isn't that cute? Who would ever
think of doing that?"

We clapped wildly when it was over and then listened to the
footsteps receding.

"Is he really going tomorrow?" I asked.

"I guess so. He has to go sometime," said Jackie as if she were
talking to herself instead of me.

"Will he be back?"

"I don't know. Let's get back in bed."

Fred did get Daddy's permission to come back by on his way
from Virginia to Texas. But he was different then somehow. Not
nearly as much fun. He didn't have time to joke with us at all.
His big brown eyes were very solemn after one talk with Jackie
sitting on the stone bench under the terrace oak. Mamma had
threatened to switch Suzanne and me if we hung around them,
but we did watch from a distance and saw Fred kiss Jackie once.
But the second time she pushed him away. I didn't know
whether to be sad for Fred or glad for me. I didn't want Jackie to
get married.

We all gathered around Fred's black Oldsmobile to see him off.
Jackie sort of half hid behind a hemlock tree as if she really
wished she weren't there, but she couldn't leave. Just as he was
about to step into his car after having said good-bye to everyone
else, Fred suddenly grabbed me and hugged me in a fierce kind
of way that was almost frightening. I knew it wasn't really my
hug and I looked around for Jackie, but she was out of sight behind the hemlock tree.

Then Fred was driving away, through a mud puddle that
splashed up over the car fenders. Daddy observed that it was
about to rain and we hurried to the house, all except Jackie who
for once didn't run, but lagged way behind. I waited for her at
the terrace steps. "He wasn't really hugging me," I said.

"You know too much," she said as she went inside.

Jackie stopped eating. Mamma couldn't persuade her to eat
anything. She would hardly talk either. She did her work and
then ran off to be by herself to dream of Fred with his dark wavy
hair, his barrel chest, and his Virginia accent.

She went to get the mail every day, and every day she came

back to the house looking as if she'd stopped along the way to be sick. Weeks went by and there was still no letter, except a very nice one from Fred's mother to Mamma thanking her for being such a sweet hostess to her son.

One day Jackie ran to the east room and threw herself on the bed shaking violently. Mamma sat beside her smoothing her hair and saying nothing except "Now, now...now, now..." Then she asked very carefully, "Do you really have any reason to be so upset, Honey? Did you and Fred have an—understanding?"

Before Jackie said anything, Mamma noticed me and sent me to see if the beans needed more water, so I missed the all-important answer.

That was the fall that Pat's baby girl, Lorna, was born, and Jackie went to stay with her and help with the baby. The letter from Texas came right after she left. It was a package, it was so thick, and there was an important "Via Air Mail" across it in Fred's smooth handwriting.

Mamma forwarded it the next day. "I wish I could see her when she gets this," she said thoughtfully with a little smile. I took it to the mailbox myself and pressed it once against my chest. After all, I thought, he did hug me, didn't he?

When Lorna was a month old, David and Pat brought Jackie home. It was so exciting seeing them and the tiny new baby; I almost forgot about Fred until I overheard Pat saying to Jackie, "Well, just be coy now, just be coy." I knew it had to be about Fred for her to be using such riddle-like words as "coy," whatever that meant.

Whenever Jackie got a letter, she glowed for about a week and would do anything we asked her from baking a cake to playing old maid cards. After that she got quieter and quieter until the next one came. Mamma spent a lot of time consoling Jackie and soothing Daddy who hated to see Jackie miserable and who threatened to "break Fred's bones" if this turned out to be a passing flirtation for him.

One day Charles and I were watching the cows at a winter grazing patch. The mailman would pass right by us on his way along our route, we realized devilishly. We laid aside our study books and waited until the mailman's black, dusty car came in sight. Then Charles hailed him and got the mail. It didn't seem such a bad thing to do until luck really smiled on us in the form of a letter to Jackie from Fred. We put all mail but that letter in the mailbox and put on super innocent faces.

Poor Jackie came back from the mailbox empty-handed and miserable. She was so sick at dinner, she couldn't even look at food. Charles kept saying things like, "You know, he doesn't have time to write to you, Jackie. He's too busy seeing all those girls out there."

"Oh, hush up!" she snapped, losing her patience. "You know that's not true."

It was two o'clock before we gave her the letter, and we both regretted having tricked her when Mamma gave us her sternest lecture. She said it was cruel to torture someone that way and that we'd be better off asleep than doing things like that. Jackie was so glad to get the letter, she forgave us instantly.

As Christmas approached Jackie knitted faster on the argyle socks she was making for Fred. She'd knit while she gave me a list of words to spell. Sometimes she'd give a word and forget to listen to see if I spelled it right. I know because I tried spelling them wrong on purpose.

There were other things for us to look for in the mail now besides Fred's letters because Christmas was coming soon. If there was a package from one of the mail order houses that said "Perishable—Keep from Heat" on the side, Jackie could read her letter to her heart's content without our teasing her. We were busy sniffing, shaking, and conjecturing.

The week before Christmas, when everything was charged with excitement, the black Oldsmobile came slowly in the driveway. Suzanne and I saw it from Pine Hill where we were speculating about a certain cedar tree, wondering if perhaps it would be the Christmas tree. We ran to meet Fred, Suzanne throwing herself into his arms as if he were John or Brantley. I hung behind a little shyly, not sure whether I was still a little girl or not.

"Where's Jackie?" Fred asked eagerly.

"She's at the house. I'll tell her you're coming," I said, and Suzanne and I took off racing up the hill. We met Jackie when we were halfway up. She was running as if feet were unnecessary. Looking behind us after she passed, we saw the two of them sort of melt together. I turned my head, suddenly embarrassed, then looked again. It was so much better than a love story in a book.

That night Jackie and Fred and Mamma and Daddy talked in the study for a long time. Charles and I kept trying to listen, but Stanley in a too-grown-up way stopped us, telling us we might get our noses pinched in the keyhole.

When the door finally opened, we crowded around. Fred was

holding Jackie's hand so tightly his knuckles were white. And Jackie was more beautiful than I'd ever seen her before, pink and shiny in the soft lamplight.

"Well, children," announced Daddy in a relieved and happy voice, "you're going to have a new brother."

There was a lot of celebrating that night, though the meal was only a simple one. It seemed as if two people that happy couldn't keep it all to themselves, and it spread into all the rest of us. There was another kind of feeling, too. It was hard to explain. But when I found Mamma crying as she chose some dishes from the cupboard, I understood just a little bit.

When Ginger came home for the holidays the next day, she and Jackie laughed and cried in each other's arms. Ginger seemed as happy helping to plan Jackie's wedding as if it were hers. Actually, she was planning hers, too, for one year later.

Fred bribed us with Mexican coins not to bother him and Jackie, but we were still nearby most of the time. He volunteered to help Jackie with the dishes. They closed the kitchen doors and took what seemed like hours doing them. But the boys discovered a tiny hole from the cellar stairwell into the kitchen where we took turns peeping until we were discovered because of Suzanne's giggles.

It was months of long waits for letters before Fred came again, this time to give Jackie a diamond ring. She'd stand in the sun just turning her hand this way and that making the ring flash colored sparks.

The wedding was in September. It was a beautiful wedding and a safe one despite Charles's threats to say "I object" during the ceremony. Jackie didn't even jump over the rail at the newel post as she'd said all along she would. She was almost as white as her dress, and it looked as if it wouldn't take much to persuade her just to run out the back door and leave it all. But she was happy afterwards. Then she was gone. All the fine guests were gone. It was just us again, minus Jackie.

After Suzanne went to sleep that night, I cried into the pillow—cried because I missed Jackie, cried because now I would be Mamma's big girl helper and I felt so small. I cried because I just wasn't sure I wanted to grow up, but I didn't want to be little anymore, either.

Three days later I got a postcard from Jackie and Fred in Bermuda. "Happy birthday!" it said. On the way to the house to help Mamma serve lunch, I took a flying trip on the cable swing.

High into a leafy dogwood I went with sky and trees melting together dizzily, then back down towards the big trunk of the pine
to which the cable was fastened, adventurously grazing my elbow as I swished past. Landing rockily on my feet, I grabbed the
card up from where I'd laid it by the tree and dashed up the hill
waving it in the air. It was the first word from our honeymooners.

Chapter Nine
Paid in Full

Within the seasons of the year there are seasons of fear, seasons of doubt, seasons of joy, seasons of fulfillment. These can come anytime and are not controlled by what time the sun rises in the mornings or what color the leaves are or even what the temperature is. There are seasons of celebration, too—maybe a day, maybe a week or more. But there can hardly be a season of celebration without preceding doubts, uncertainties, fears, and hard work.

The ridge, running along the western side of Pinedale, might not be ours for long according to overheard conversations between Mamma and Daddy. Charles pointed out that they had talked like that for years, and Stanley said that the land between the highway and the river used to be part of Pinedale, but it had been sold when the mortgage payments became too hard to get together. *Mortgage* was a word that was hard to understand. Maybe I had it confused with *morgue.* Anyway, I hated the word, because it meant things weren't just right. It meant the ridge might become populated with a row of "matchbox" houses as Daddy called them.

It was on the ridge that King and Queen Pine stood so proudly. They were several feet taller than any of the trees around them, and they stood close together. When you walked home from town they were the first to greet you, their pointed tops reaching into the sky. If you were standing next to them, they didn't seem nearly so tall. But from the highway they were the royalty of the woods.

On the steep north end of the ridge above the waiting wall (a stone wall built into the driveway bank—a lovely violet-covered place to wait for the mailman or buses), there was thick, soft moss under a dogwood tree. If you sat down for even a little while, you could see the print of yourself when you stood up. All the miniature moss trees would be temporarily flattened over. It was a perfect place for Cinderella's ball, complete with carpet, atmosphere, hidden concertos, and a host of imaginary dancers.

On a Sunday afternoon a quiet activity, less likely to get us into mischief than some, was lying just inside the fence at the cliff side of the ridge watching the cars go by. We could see, but could not be seen. It was fun to make up stories about the people who went by. Of course we couldn't really see much except the tops of the cars, glimpses of Sunday hats, shirted arms, or rounded, suntanned arms which brought low whistles from the boys.

The glimpses were food for wild imaginations. Stanley was so graphic in his description of a mother and father on their way to a far-off hospital to see their wounded soldier boy that I never was quite sure whether he really knew the people. But all that I had seen go by was a lady who reached up with a gloved hand to dab at her face with a handkerchief.

There was one place along the ridge where the eastern side dipped down to the brook with a breathless steepness. It was way up the brook from the pond where there were a lot of oak trees. With pieces of old grocery boxes we sledded and skated on the slick leaves, always getting stopped barely short of the brook, well, almost always.

The ridge was a really nice place to be if there were someone with you. I didn't like to go there alone partly because of the packs of dogs that came there to tree squirrels. I wasn't always sure what their intentions were; besides, it just wasn't quite home. The eastern side of the brook was home, the western side was a place of adventure, but not one where you would want to find yourself after dark.

It seemed to me that whenever money matters came up, Daddy got a headache and had to splash water on his forehead to cool his temples. Of course money had to be mentioned, and so Daddy had an awful lot of headaches. He also spent a lot of time pacing the Hall floor, back and forth, muttering things about being useless: "If a man cannot work, neither should he eat." Sometimes he'd get the horsehair broom from the head of the cellar steps and begin sweeping with long vigorous strokes. "Don't tell anyone up town that you saw your Dad sweeping the floor," he'd say.

Stanley went to work at a bank in Atlanta. He was eighteen and ready to start out on his own. But to me, home wouldn't be the same without him. I'd miss his and Charles's quarreling and their lively evening sessions with guitar and fiddle. I'd miss his brotherly counsel, too, his reassurances when the world seemed to be all unfairness and cruelty to a girl just entering her teens. It was hard to sing in our farewell circle the day he left. My throat hurt so trying to say, "Till we mee-e-et, till we me-e-et, God be with you till we meet again." Mamma cried as she did every time one of her children made their first break from home.

Stanley did come home often on weekends, either hitchhiking or riding the bus. But it was never quite the same again. He never had time again to watch the cars from the ridge or to slide down the leafy slope. He and Charles no longer took turns swinging the grapevine across the brook.

Those who had jobs away from home, now periodically sent checks to help at Pinedale, either chipping away at ridge payments, or buying a bucket of peanut butter and a bag of sugar. Not that I knew much about those offerings. But sometimes I did notice Mamma tucking a check into the front of her dress before she'd read a letter to us.

It was always fun to go for the mail, to try to guess what all the pieces were. We never left any packets unturned, outgoing or incoming. So of course we noticed the thick envelopes from different magazines like the *Country Gentleman* magazine. The funny thing was that they weren't always from the magazines, but also to them, those brown manila envelopes. And the ones from *Saturday Evening Post, Audubon*, and other magazines, were addressed in Mamma's handwriting to Daddy, though Mamma had been right there at home, certainly hadn't been to New York, Philadelphia, or someplace like that.

Mamma and Daddy didn't talk about what was in those envelopes in front of us, but it always happened that Daddy was very depressed after getting one. For two or three days he wouldn't even try to put shaving cream on Suzanne's and my necks as he shaved, a playful trick of his that we pretended to despise.

There were threats of the highway's being widened. A man in a gray hat with a tiny feather in the band walked up the spring vista one day and knocked loudly at the door. He made some kind of offer. He talked pretty low, and I couldn't hear him from up on the balcony. But Daddy's reply was not hard to hear. "I don't care what you offer," came the voice of hot steel, "The land is not for sale, Highways are an abomination to mankind. Years from now there will be concrete from town to town, but this place is going to be here. There is going to be one place where folks can see the land as the Lord made it."

"But, sir…"

"That's the end of it. Until I'm forced, there is no sale."

There was the sound of an empty chair rocking back and forth and the sound of the west door opening.

"Good day, sir," I heard Daddy say and, running to a west window, I saw the man shaking his head as he started back down the hill. Downstairs Daddy was muttering out loud as he cleaned an ash tray the man had used.

Charles brought the mail up the day the letter from *Audobon* magazine arrived, a thin letter, not a thick envelope. The address was typewritten, and there was a special postmark that said, "Save our Animals." When Charles laid the mail on the breakfast table, Mamma came from the kitchen, wiping her hands on her apron.

Spying that letter on top of the mail, she grabbed it and ripped it open, not carefully prying the flap up as she usually did. "Floyd, they're accepting your article at *Audobon*. Oh, isn't that wonderful? They want to use the picture of our house, too."

It was the first time I had ever seen Mamma quite that excited. She looked as if she might dance. Daddy came out of his study, his mustache twitching, his eyes twinkling behind his glasses as they used to do. "Well, well," he said, straightening his shoulders, "when is the date?"

"It says April of next year. What a long time to wait!"

"Well, that's the way magazines operate, planning months ahead. And that will be a good month for a little article on birds nesting in the ivy."

After that Mamma hummed little songs while she worked, even though the ridge payment still had not been made. There was still a bill at the grocery store and one at the hardware for new fencing material, but Daddy had his fighting spirit back. Maybe the little article was nothing like the ones he used to type out regularly for *Atlanta Journal*, still it gave him a sense of well being he'd sorely missed. Somehow, things *would* work out.

Some months later John arranged his business so that he could be at Pinedale on a Monday morning and take Daddy to town. Mamma said Daddy used to do all the business in town, even buy the groceries for her, but I couldn't remember that. It seemed strange to me for him to be going to town on business that Monday. He was dressed in his dark gray suit, and he truly looked kingly as he stepped out the door and into John's car. He was wearing his Stetson hat instead of his everyday helmet.

I asked Mamma what he was going to do. "He's going to sign some papers," she said vaguely.

Charles knew more about it than I did, but he wouldn't talk. "It's just business. Girls don't understand about business deals."

Maybe I couldn't understand a business deal. But I knew the feeling in the air when something different was about to happen.

I was washing the west windows when John and Daddy came home. Daddy got out of the car and reached back in for a little brown bag. In his other hand was a long white envelope. As he stepped lightly in the front door I heard him say, "Well, Eula, King and Queen Pine have never looked so good. They're really ours now. After twenty years!"

"Oh, that's good!" Mamma said simply, and there was a relief born out of years of worry in her voice.

I jumped down from the window ledge as Daddy called, "Come here, children!"

He opened the brown bag and passed it to each of us. A chocolate bar for every one of us! A whole chocolate bar! It was a perfect way of celebrating. What could be more special than having your own chocolate bar which you didn't have to divide into so many squares to make it go around?

That night as the sun was going down behind the ridge, Mamma and Daddy went for a walk. They were swinging hands as they went down the west vista, and Daddy was whistling "The Missouri Waltz."

Chapter Ten
Mamma and Daddy Go Traveling

The trip had been planned for a long time. As long as I could remember, Daddy and Mamma had talked of someday going to New England and Canada. Daddy longed to see England, but he never had the opportunity, though he had that nice space between his teeth which superstition said earned him a sea voyage. New England was his second choice.

It was to be a trip of a lifetime for them. They had been to New York on their honeymoon in the twenties. They called it their honeymoon, though they already had Orman at the time and Grandma went along to help take care of him. Also, Daddy had business contacts to make in New York. Since then all their long trips had been taken apart from each other. Someone always had to stay at home with the young children, the cows, and the dogs. Even now they were uneasy about leaving Charles, Suzanne, and me alone for so long (two whole weeks), but we assured them we'd be all right. Charles was seventeen, I was fourteen, and Suzanne was ten. A close neighbor, Ray Nicholson, would check on us daily to be sure we were all right. Ray and Kathleen and their little girls Tricia and Kathy lived on the other side of the highway, up the hill from our mailbox. They were at one time proprietors of the gas station and, along with his mother and the rest of a large family of Nicholsons, were glad to help out any time. The nice thing about Ray was he always seemed so happy, never let a cloud overcome the big smile which lit his tanned face.

Stanley, who had a two-weeks vacation from his job at Arrendale's, was ready to go, and Daddy as usual was rushing Mamma. She kept going back in the house to do one more little thing. Finally they were getting in the car, Daddy in the front

with Stan, Mamma in back. She turned again as Daddy held the
door for her and hugged us all three real tight as if she hadn't already.

"Take care now, children," Daddy said as he folded his long
legs into Stan's car. He had on his faithful pith helmet and had a
piece of cardboard to use for a sun shield. The sun was scalding
bright right then. It even hurt my eyes.

"We'll send you a card," Mamma called, and the car backed
around to turn at the holly. We stood on the west steps and
waved to them as they crossed the pond view at the bottom of
the hill. We weren't even admitting to ourselves how awesome
and exciting an occasion this was: to be left with the responsibility—and freedom—of the whole place.

As the car disappeared around the last glimpsing place, my
hand fell to my side. *I'm the lady of the house,* I thought. It was
wonderful and frightening, too. The afternoon suddenly seemed
like a long stretch in front of us since it was only two o'clock
then.

Charles said there was a patch of weeds he wanted to cut
down in the grove. I went in the house to see what surprise job I
would tackle first. Mamma had said just to take care of the cow's
milk, cook, and try to keep up with my lessons. "That'll be
enough," she said anxiously, "since the cow's fresh and you'll
have to churn, too." But it didn't sound nearly interesting
enough.

The house felt odd as I walked through the Hall and stood in-
decisively in the breakfast room. To my right was Daddy's study
with its smoke-stained curtains. (He was always putting a log in
the fire that was too long and stuck way out in the room.
Mamma said he must really like smoke in his eyes.) To my left
was the corridor and the kitchen, dark because of the ivy hanging over the northern window. It wasn't late enough for the sun
to be coming in the little western window over the stairs. Directly in front of me was the breakfast table which hadn't been
used for a breakfast table in years. It was piled high with stacks
of books, old mail, and so forth. Mamma would really be happy
if I cleaned that off, but I wasn't in the right mood. I wasn't sure
what mood I was in. The house seemed the same as usual, but
the hairs on my arms were standing on end and even my scalp
felt crawly the way it did when we read the *Hound of the Baskervilles.*

Should I wash Daddy's curtains? They were so dirty, I couldn't tell what they were supposed to look like. I tried to picture how they'd look all white and bright. Something about the outdoors willed my eyes to turn back to the breakfast room window. I shuddered. There was a strange yellow light outdoors. It wasn't coming from any particular direction like sunshine; it was everywhere. It seemed thick enough to feel, like a fabric, but it didn't make any shadows. Where was the scalding sunshine of a few minutes ago?

Taking a step down into Daddy's study, I tip-toed for no reason across his slate floor, put one knee on the edge of Daddy's bed ready to climb across and take down the curtains. Suzanne's scream arrested me.

"We've got to get in the cellar," Charles said breathlessly, slamming the west door behind him.

I didn't even know how I got out of the study. We followed Charles down the damp cellar steps without stopping to ask why. In the musty, earthen hole we could only feel each other as we huddled in a knot. The dark was panicky thick. "What is it?" I asked, but I couldn't even hear my own question because of the roar that came rolling over the house. It was like having a hundred trains wreck while you hide under a bridge. We clung together, and I wondered in a flash how long it would be before someone found our bodies.

But then as quickly as it had come it was all over. We crept out into the light and were amazed to find the house quite whole and peaceful with only a soft patter of rain beginning to sound on the roof. We looked from all the windows and saw only a few limbs fallen, nothing disastrous at all. Soon even the rain stopped and the sun came back out bright as ever.

"There must be some damage somewhere," Charles said. "I'd better go see."

Of course we went with him. It was only three o'clock, just one hour since the folks left on their trip. "They'll be back," Charles predicted. "You know Daddy will never go now." It seemed sad they weren't going to have their trip.

The tornado had hit Pine Hill, uprooting giant pine trees and laying them across each other in a crazy manner. It was impossible to imagine the strength of something that could pick trees up like that, twist them, and lay them down as if they were no bigger than the sticks we once used to build tiny houses. "I'll talk to Ray Nicholson tomorrow. We need to start sawing this up," Charles said, measuring the timber with his eyes.

"But what if Daddy doesn't come back?"

"We'll still have to start cutting. We can't wait two weeks to begin. The beetles would get in the wood."

"But you and Ray can't do it by yourselves with Daddy not even here."

"Well, we can, too," retorted Charles. "What do you think Dad is anyway? Some kind of god? I know how he wants things done."

Charles kicked at the fan-shaped root system of a fallen pine, and loose dirt fell skittering into the fresh hole.

It was true, I thought. I really did think Daddy was an arm of God and that without him nothing really important could be done. He was a guard by whom nothing harmful could pass. He fed us on truth, telling us about evil as he threw it out. He or Mamma was always there. That's why the afternoon seemed so strange, not because of the tornado, but because of the absence of security. There was no one to say, "This is what has happened. This is what shall be done about it. That settles it." But Charles was doing a pretty good job at it.

We didn't mention again whether or not the folks would be coming back, but we all three kept looking down the driveway from time to time until it was dark. Then we locked up tight and lit the lamps. There was a lonesomeness lurking in the shadows which we tried to keep away with our loud talking and arguing, but it seemed our voices got quieter and quieter. Later we learned that the folks had gotten out of reach of the local radio station by the time the tornado came, and the only bad weather that came near them was a rain which, Daddy remarked, would be good for Pinedale.

The next day Charles took the power saw and, with Ray's help, began cutting the timber. I took down the curtains early so I could get them washed and back up by night. Suzanne had gone out happily to mow Myrtle Lawn with our rotary mower. She was happy anytime that Lassie, her collie pup which she had gotten for Christmas, was running along at her heels.

We had decided that morning over breakfast (a choice of three kinds of dry cereals, a treat Mamma had taken pleasure in supplying us with) that we would all work very hard this first week and get everything in tip-top shape. Then we would do just what we wanted to do the second week. As I scrubbed the curtains, putting them through one water after another, I planned my next project. I would start washing windows. I might even wash all of

STONE GABLES

them—that is, if I ever got through with these curtains. Mamma had said she needed new curtains in the study and she hadn't said it for nothing! They refused to be white—or whatever they'd been—again.

Finally I did what I'd seen Mamma do with stubborn stains. I located a gallon jug of bleach and poured some in on the curtains, a nice generous amount for a generous stain. Leaving the dark mass soaking, I began to prepare lunch.

Cookery, it seemed, was as unflattering, unglamorous a job as laundering was. The pancakes over slices of potted meat were burned and raw at the same time. Not even Lassie liked them. The beans were scorched because they'd cooked in sudden spurts of heat as I remembered to put wood in the fire. Suzanne helped pick all the scorched ones out, but they still tasted bad. We resorted to creamy milk over cereal and gorged ourselves.

Midafternoon found the curtains eaten to shreds and still quite dingy. I hung them on the line and looked sadly at my red knuckles. Suzanne thought it was terribly funny for some reason, which didn't help my feelings at all. "Why don't you just bury them?" she giggled. "I wouldn't even want them for Lassie's bed."

It took three hours that night to get all the milk put away; there was so much left from the morning milking that all the containers were full, even though Ray had taken a gallon home with him. In desperation Suzanne and I gave Lassie a great dish full to drink. After lapping it all up, she promptly lost it all over the kitchen floor. Suzanne was terribly upset and spent her time comforting Lassie while I cleaned up the mess, my stomach lurching.

It didn't take many days to teach me that a "fresh" cow is no laughing matter. I saved the milk in a big crock, let the cream rise, warmed it by a corner of the stove, and churned—and churned and churned some more! When butter finally came I washed it as I'd seen Mamma do and made patties. We gave milk to Ray every day, drank it, ate bread in it, fed it to everything living, including the birds. And there was still milk. I decided the Milky Way probably was created when a couple went on a trip and left their "fresh" cow with their children.

One night while we were in the study, each absorbed in a book, there was a scraping sound outside the south door, a very seldom used door. We all heard it and looked at each other with widened eyes. But none of us said anything. Lassie, lying at

Suzanne's feet, whined and stirred, then lay still again, her long slender nose across her paws. Crusoe and Thor began to bark outside.

Charles returned to his government book and I to my history, but my mind was not on the founding of the colonies at all. I shivered and rubbed the sudden chill bumps on my arms. Peering over my book I saw that Suzanne wasn't studying either. About that time there was a light rap at the west door after which Thor barked furiously.

Charles closed his book and looked quickly at Dad's .22 rifle on the wall. His adam's apple went up and down as he swallowed.

"Maybe somebody just wants to see us," I whispered through dry lips.

"They wouldn't be so sneaky if they were up to any good," said Charles. "They'd use the doorknocker."

The knock came again, and immediately someone tried the knob. Charles stood and got the gun off the wall.

"Lock the study door behind me when I go out," he said.

My hand shook as I pushed the lock to. Suzanne had tears welling in her eyes.

"Don't worry," I said, trying to make my voice sound steady. "Where's Lassie?"

"I let her go with Charles. She might be able to help," she said with a catch in her voice.

Charles's steps were barely audible as he neared the west door. There hadn't been another sound from outside except the chorus of tree frogs and the wild barking of the two dogs. Whoever it was might have gone to another door by now. I hoped he would get tangled up in Daddy's lime hedge planted under the windows. The thorns were long and treacherous and were loaded with poison like yellow jackets.

Leaning against the door, I closed my eyes tight and prayed as hard as I knew how—not sentences, just a desperate jumble of thought-pleas that only God could understand. I opened my eyes as I heard the west door open and Charles call out bravely, "Who's there? I say, who's there?"

There was no answer. But we heard Lassie growl deep down in her throat. Suzanne's face brightened. "Good girl," she whispered. "She won't let anyone attack Charles."

The door closed then, but we couldn't tell whether Charles had gone out or in. We couldn't hear anything. Other dogs began to bark not far away. Thor and Crusoe answered them, barking and growling intermittently.

Then there were swishing footsteps in the myrtle outside the study windows. It sure was good we'd put that sheet up in place of the ruined curtains. Suzanne grabbed my arm and held it so tightly it hurt. My chest hurt, too, my heart was beating so. If only I could look over at Daddy's bed and see him there resting the back of his head in his hands, his feet propped up on the footboard. But he was hundreds of miles away, and the footsteps were right past the hedge now and I wasn't sure they'd stop.

Then a hoarse whisper reached us from outside. "Brenda, go to the door and let me in. Quick! I'm locked out." I was so relieved to hear Charles, my knees went limp and my feet wouldn't move. "Go on, hurry!" he urged with no small irritation.

Finally I found myself unlocking the study door and walking across the Hall towards the west door. Even the rocking chairs with comforters slung over their backs looked as if they were hiding something evil. I imagined there were eyes gleaming from the Louis XIV chair.

"Charles?" I whispered at the door and then opened it quickly as I heard his impatient answer.

"Boy, you were slow!" he exclaimed. "Someone could have beaten me to a pulp before you'd get around to letting me in."

"Is he gone?"

"Reckon so. No one would ever answer me. The dogs scared him off, I guess. That is, if there was really someone there."

"Well, you know there was," I said as we walked in the study.

"Where's Lassie, where's my Lassie? I sent her to help you, and you've just left her out there for some mean ole man to shoot," Suzanne cried hysterically.

Charles took her by the shoulders and shook her. "Listen! Listen to me! Lassie's okay. I'll go back and get her. Just hold on now."

She continued to sob and shake as Charles went back to let the eager Lassie in. As she fondled Lassie's silky ears, Suzanne whispered, "Good girl, good ole girl."

"You care more about Lassie than you do about me," said Charles morosely.

Surprisingly, we all slept well that night, and the next morning everything looked normal and right again. As I came down the stairs, I thought how comfortable and natural the rocking chairs looked in daylight. There were strange footprints outside, though, to prove we hadn't just imagined everything.

By the end of the week Charles had the logs ready to snake together. Suzanne had mowed all the lawns. And I felt as if I had milk running out my ears. The only surprise I had for Mamma so far was a clean kitchen window and three ruined curtains.

There were postcards for each of us on Saturday. We showed them to Ray when he came to check on us. They were mailed in Ipswich, Massachusetts—such an English-sounding place. Mamma said on Charles's card that they had met a Cogswell lady and had a wonderful time tracing family lines, discovering that hers and Daddy's families were connected back in England. Charles's middle name is Cogswell, so she thought it would be interesting to him. Down at the very bottom squeezed around the printing on the card, Mamma had written, "I miss you all!"

On Sunday after church I proudly served a banana pudding with dinner. Charles winked at Suzanne and said, "She's finally improving, isn't she?"

Suzanne giggled. "Yep. She sure is."

I didn't bother telling them it was made from instant pudding, not boiled like Mamma's.

We'd been alone a week and we seemed to be accustomed now to living by ourselves. We had a handle on the chores and had woven new routines into our days. It didn't seem quite as gloomy when night fell thickly and suddenly down through the pines that Sunday night. We failed to light the stairway lamp before dark, but Charles went creeping up the stairs to do it, and I told myself I could have done it if he hadn't.

Before we went to bed we made plans for a beautiful day Monday, the beginning of our wonderful second week when we would take time to play. After lessons in the morning, we would have a picnic and each read in a favorite book. Maybe I would even write a poem. The thought made a tickle of anticipation run through my fingers. Charles would work on a treasured invention of his; Suzanne and I would hunt birds' nests and visit our favorite woodsy haunts. And come nightfall we would listen to all the hillbilly music we wanted to on Daddy's radio, even turn it up loud. I don't think it occurred to us to turn the radio on that Sunday night. Dad's displeasure at playing such music would have been even stronger on Sunday and the radio was in his room, surrounded by his scent, his old field coat hanging on a hook, his work shoes stashed under the bed.

The next morning I wakened knowing I had heard something, but not knowing what. There was nothing but the sound of birds outside and the even breathing of Suzanne beside me. Then it came again, the sound of the doorknocker crashing against its plate "Wham, wham, wham." It couldn't be, I thought, but it sure does sound commanding just like...

As my feet touched the floor I heard Charles grabbing his door open. My heart pounded against my ribs as he took the stairs two or three at a time. Quickly I pulled on my dress. It couldn't be Daddy's knock, no matter how much it sounded like it. So who was it? Who could be coming so early in the morning?

Then I knew. We all knew. Daddy's loud laughter filled the whole house. But who else did we hear? Children's voices! Pat's voice! Here she came up the stairs to find us, her smile so confidently cheerful, her hair so shiny and healthy. Her sparkling eyes certainly didn't show she'd been traveling all night, but that's what they'd done.

The folks had stopped to see Jackie and Fred in Towson, Maryland, on their way and had returned by Pat and David's home in Charleston, West Virginia. And had brought Pat and the children to stay a week or two until David came for them. Wonder of wonders!

"Oh, it's so good to be here!" Pat cried urging us down the stairs. A quiet two-year-old Lorna climbed to meet us and behind her Stan carried curly-headed baby Robert. Our squeals of excitement brought looks of awe on the children's faces.

Between building a fire in the kitchen and "scratching together" some breakfast, Mamma surveyed the whole house, not really as if she were looking for something to be wrong, just wanting to see everything, touch a chair back here, a picture frame there assuring herself, I guess, that she really was home. She hardly even blinked when she saw the sheet over Daddy's windows.

"Good riddance," she murmured. "Did you have any trouble with anything, honey?"

"N-no. Nothing at all. Except the tornado."

"Have plenty of milk?"

"Oh, yes! Gallons and gallons!"

She smiled as she headed back to the kitchen. "Help me get breakfast on," she said.

We'd decided not to tell the folks about our strange night visitor. It would be silly for them to worry about something that was over and done, Charles said. The tornado damage was enough bad news.

Daddy had seen the wreckage on Pine Hill as they drove in. But he was so glad to be home, he simply couldn't let it put him into a morose mood. Instead, everything near him seemed to vibrate, and he almost choked us with his hugs. Stanley and Mamma had enjoyed the trip, as much as they could with Daddy wanting to come back ever since they got to New England. He couldn't stand to be gone a second week, Mamma said. She didn't seem at all sad to be back, either. "All these years they wanted to take that trip, then they couldn't wait to get back home," grumbled Stanley who really had wanted to see more of the world.

All day Daddy kept bursting into song: "The hills of home, the hills of h-o-ome." It was really good to have the noise of people, lots of people, in the house again. I didn't mind going up to light the lamp that night even in the dark, because I could hear the sounds of Daddy's newscast and a stove lid rattling authoritatively in the kitchen.

Chapter Eleven
Can They See the Same Moon?

The bees were beginning to hum sleepily in the heavy ivy that hung in clumps from the parapet around the kitchen roof. It was just after dinner on a spring day. The bees never started humming until about dinner time, or if they did, everyone was too busy to hear them—especially today.

It was an extra busy day with much to do besides the normal business of learning lessons, feeding chickens, milking the cow, churning, making up beds, and sweeping the kitchen floor. There was company to prepare for. Company? No, Brantley and Helen weren't company. They were much more important than company, because the way they saw us today might be the way they remembered us for five years.

I walked around the garage to a privet tree where Daddy had hung two beheaded chickens by their feet to bleed. The heavy scent of privets in bloom couldn't come near to erasing the smell of blood. Mamma had sent me to see if they were about to stop dripping. I shuddered at the sight of blood-stained wood chips on the ground and noted that the drops now fell few and far between. Mamma said her mother always wrung a chicken's neck, but she never could. So Daddy chopped their heads off which seemed far worse to me. It was an operation I always tried to avoid, but several times I had seen the beheaded chickens flapping around before Daddy got them tied up. He explained that they were really dead and, without a head, could feel no pain. But what about all the other chickens half-lifting their wings and running around in circles cackling wildly? Did they have a name for the chicken-friend they'd just lost?

As I started back inside, a mockingbird began an ecstatic sonata in the crab apple tree. My hand on the cool doorknob, I

stood a minute listening. Mockingbirds knew nothing of long farewells; their sadnesses, like the chickens', lasted only minutes and then they were singing again. This time tomorrow, I thought, Brantley will be on his way across the country to board a ship in Seattle.

I was dusting the rooms upstairs when Suzanne called out that they were coming. We raced down the stairs and down the terrace to meet them, each one wanting to hold one-year-old Joy who really preferred that neither of us hold her. Phillip asked to see the cow and Suzanne took him to the pasture.

"Hello, Mom," Brantley was saying as he hugged her and planted a hard kiss on her forehead.

"Good to see you, son," Dad laughed as Brantley nursed his hand after their hard clasp.

"Dad, you can still out-grip me, and you're twice as old as I."

Helen rolled up her pretty blue sleeves to help in the kitchen; Joy finally consented to my holding her as long as we stayed out of her mother's sight. I looked at her chubby legs and her blonde baby hair and wondered what she could look like in five years when they came back from Japan.

Japan! A place of strange music, straw mats, and foreign language—a place that looked like a little orange boot on our school map. Japan—where the people had black straight hair and slanted eyes. At least, that was what the Japanese paper dolls were like that Suzanne and I had made. We had gotten the pattern out of our big red *Home Toy Shop* book. With black yarn for hair and scraps of silk for long kimonos, they looked very Japanese to us. I thought about giving mine to Joy to play with, but she would try to eat it.

John had been to Japan when he was in the Army. That's where he was when he had a wreck in a jeep while chauffeuring a colonel or something. He'd broken his leg and he said it still hurt on rainy days. But worse than the wreck was the time he had polio. It wasn't the crippling kind, but the kind that killed you fast if it were going to. Vaguely I could remember the long days of waiting to hear from John.

Mamma had someone wait for the mail every day in case there were a special delivery letter. Daddy paced the floor and did not whistle. The day the letter did come that said John was going to get well, Mamma sat down by the kitchen stove and cried.

I remembered my little bead necklace John had brought me when he came home, and I took Joy with me upstairs to look at it. It was a delicate flowery necklace made with a zillion tiny blue and white beads. It had just fitted me when John gave it to me, but now was far too small. I was his little "pow-wow girl" then, and oh, how tall he was when he came home! He had to bend his head a little coming in the kitchen door, or so it seemed to me. Mamma said he wasn't taller, just thinner.

Joy tried to get hold of the necklace as I fastened it around her little neck, and then she began to cry because she couldn't see it. Laying it carefully back in my "secret" drawer (one of the two little raised drawers on either side of a marble-topped dresser, a place I had inherited when Ginger went off to school), I put her on my shoulders. "Let's go see the cow," I said.

When we came back from the pasture, Brantley was helping Mamma pull out the second leaf on the dining table. "These things stick so when the weather is damp," Mamma explained. "But we need the whole table. John and Betty and the children will be here soon."

"That's good. I'm glad they live right over the hill from you now. Their new house Maple Bend sure is nice." Brantley began buttoning and unbuttoning the cuff of his shirt as if he were trying to think what else to say. Then abruptly he asked, "Is the weed cutter in the garage?"

"Yes. Right there in the tool corner. But you don't need to..."

"I'm just going to knock down a few weeds around Myrtle Lawn. I won't be long."

When he came back there was redness at the corners of his eyes, and his glasses were especially shiny as if he'd just wiped them. But his smile was wide and genuine. He's just been to tell Pinedale good-bye, I thought, and wondered how he could. Being a foreign missionary required sacrifices I'd never realized before.

Dinner that night was gay and noisy. We usually called the evening meal supper, but that night it was dinner. The chickens had become a huge chicken salad. Betty had brought sliced ham and deviled eggs. There were green beans, potato salad, hot cornbread with fresh butter, and turnip greens. Steaming on the buffet was a deep-dish blackberry pie made with the last two jars of last year's berries. It was one of Brantley's favorites.

Helen laughed as she took a helping of potato salad. "Mom, do you remember when I first came here to visit? Remember that tremendous potato salad you made? I wondered why you had made so much, and I was scared to eat anything."

Mamma laughed with her. "It wasn't because of you we made such a big salad. It was because of us. It was nearly all eaten, too, nearly the whole dishpan full."

"Dishpan!" exclaimed Charles.

"Yes. What could possibly be any cleaner?"

"Ugh!"

There was the clink of silver against china, little thuds as glasses were set down, lively conversations, sudden silences, a throat-clearing, a child spilling his juice on the stairs, Mamma sending me to clean it up—and all the sounds punctuated with bursts of laughter over little nothings.

It really wasn't that different from other family gatherings. It should be, I thought. There should be some way of making it special. When someone left for five years, was there nothing more you could do than eat together and then say goodbye? At the same time, I dreaded the evening service because I knew I would get all chokey inside.

There were reddish sunset bars falling through the blinds as we got up from the table. "Let's leave the dishes this time, girls," Mamma said.

"It would be nice to sit on the steps and watch the sun go down," Brantley said quietly.

Suzanne and I frolicked with the children—Brantley's Phillip and John's Emily, Joan, and Paul—on the terrace. We played "Rover, red Rover," "Catch a fellow off a stone," and just plain running. Dew dampened the grass and our feet slid on sharp turns. Phillip and Paul found that to be as good a game as any, sliding and falling amongst hilarious laughter. Even baby Carol in Betty's lap crowed in delight and clapped her little hands.

Helen held Joy's hands and let her walk back and forth at the foot of the steps. "She can almost walk, but it's going to be hard to learn on board ship, I guess," she said.

"Maybe it's a good thing she's not walking yet. It will be hard as it is to keep up with her and be sure she doesn't get too close to the edge of the deck. It gives me cold chills to think of one of them going overboard!" Mamma rubbed her arms.

"Oh, but, Mom, they'll give us halters for the children. You needn't worry one minute. They'll be just fine."

"Eula, I can't believe this is the fellow who used to feed his math book to the cow. Can you?" Daddy slapped Brantley heartily on the back.

"Nor the one who missed a ride with you to town because he

was too busy watching an ant hill," Mamma said, shaking her head.

"Have you forgotten the time I deliberately broke a hoe so I wouldn't have to work?" Brantley prodded.

"The sinner knows his own transgressions," laughed Daddy.

It was hard to imagine Brantley being little and doing those things. I could close my eyes and see a picture of him and John, Orman and Pat, and Ginger when they were little. The boys had their hair cut with bangs and wore cut-off overalls. Blonde-haired Ginger was holding to a corner of her dress. They all had camera-fixed smiles except John who looked as if he had been called from something much more interesting. Somehow I didn't really believe that the children in that picture were the same ones that I knew grown-up. But it was comforting to know they had been naughty, too!

It was getting dusky. Fireflies, like misplaced planets, blinked here and there. There was a sense of urgency in the air. Even though Helen and Betty were exchanging recipes and the boys were discussing the aesthetic qualities in the chromed lines of new cars, everyone knew that Brantley would have to leave soon to go back to Atlanta for an early start cross-country next day.

Daddy cleared his throat to speak, but before he could say anything, Brantley sprang up, pulling Helen with him. "We're going to sing a song for you before we go," he said.

Even the children hushed as the harmonious strains of "How Great Thou Art" trembled in the dampening air. Brantley had his arm around Helen as they sang. "Then sings my soul, my Saviour God to thee..." I knew I would always remember the way they looked then—Helen with her curly black hair falling over her long-sleeved blue dress with lace and tiny buttons down the front, Brantley with a touch of gray in his hair, yet a boyish curl falling on his forehead. I knew I would remember that look of peace in their faces, that look of joy mixed with momentary sadness. "When I look down from lofty mountain grandeur...How great Thou art, how great Thou art!"

It was during Daddy's prayer that Mamma started to cry. I knew she didn't want to cry because she had told me so as we washed turnip greens together. "No one likes to leave with someone crying," she'd said. "It just makes it harder. I would like to be able to smile when I wave good-bye."

But now she was pulling a handkerchief from her bosom. I didn't have to look to know because I was sitting right beside

her. That's how I knew when Daddy slipped his arm around her. His hand ran into my shoulder I was so close. "Almighty God, take care of our boy...your boy...and his family. In all their journeys watch over them...Amen."

As they piled into their car we showered them with merry goodbyes as if we'd be seeing each other again in a month or two. Brantley accelerated a time or two making sure the motor didn't stall. Daddy said, "Hope you don't burn something up." Brantley smiled broadly at the old joke. Mamma was able to smile as she waved. And then they were gone, backing around beside the big holly, rocking down the uneven road, tooting the horn in response to our waving as they crossed the pond vista. As we watched for the last glimpse of red tail lights, I was conscious still of the rib-cracking hug Brantley had given me.

After John, Betty, and their children had started back to Maple Bend, and everyone else had gone inside, Suzanne and I tried to find the big dipper in an open, starry sky. We could always find the little dipper, but the big one was sometimes hard to distinguish. "Can they really see the same moon over in Japan?" Suzanne wondered aloud.

"Why, of course," I answered as if I could comprehend the hugeness of the world with no effort.

As we walked to the door, a breeze riffled through the spring-touched branches of the oak by the steps. It was as if the tree had absorbed Brantley's and Helen's song and would play it now whenever the wind came through: "Then sings my soul...how great Thou art!"

Chapter Twelve
From Wicks to Switches

It was the day of all days that we dreamed of—the day the electricity was to be turned on. Daddy still wasn't happy about it and had made the final arrangements only so that Mamma could have an electric range. Many times we had talked of "when we get electric lights, we'll..." But it had been an almost hopeless dream that at times faded into the background like the image of the tower that never was.

Daddy had planned when the rest of the house was completed to build a tower at the back of the house connected to the garage. But the Depression had come. It was hard to get men to work because they had gone to Florida and elsewhere seeking higher wages. The tower had been postponed until there was help, then postponed because of Daddy's health, postponed again and again. Occasionally he still mentioned it, but only as something he wished he could have done, not as something he was going to do. He sometimes reflected that if he had built the tower he would be able to climb up the three or four stories and look out at the mountains. Mamma mentioned a few times how one of the rooms in the tower was to have been an extra bedroom, and that she would like to have had a room with four rubber walls where she could put us when we were noisy and quarrelsome.

The electricity was like a has-been dream many times, too. "If we had finished having the house wired..."; "I always meant eventually to have a good furnace under the nice iron grate in the Hall floor." (In the meantime, we just swept trash through the grate down into the cellar. The cellar wasn't floored and it was so handy—when Mamma wasn't looking.)

It didn't matter to Daddy, of course, that everyone else in Habersham County had electricity already. But it mattered to us.

We were embarrassed to have friends visit us at night because they were so fascinated by our kerosene lamps, making us feel like part of an antique museum.

Brantley had worked on the wiring as had Stanley, Charles, and then an electrician from Clarkesville who said it was ready. Finally it was time to see about getting the electric company to put a line to our house. There was excitement running rampant at mealtimes those days because we were sure it was finally happening. But when Daddy learned how much it would cost to have the line run so far into our woods and also how much the landscape would be affected, suddenly the whole thing was dropped.

No electricity. The wall sockets were wired to the outside of concrete walls (even though Daddy had had some wires embedded in walls when he built the house). There were light fixtures grinning down at us from the ceiling as if to say, "Try me. Don't I look as if I would work?" But it seemed we wouldn't have the power that would make things turn on.

Then one day Daddy and a man from the electric company went for a walk toward the garden and the Switch Field. He said they could come in that way instead of from the front and it wouldn't be quite as expensive. But they would still have to cut a lot of trees.

Daddy and Mamma talked for days about the possibility, or was it weeks? They went for walks in the evening, studying the path the wires would take. It seemed that Daddy was having a real battle within himself, wanting to give Mamma the things she needed, but at the same time hurting at the thought of having the wide path cut. "Wires are ugly scars across the face of the earth," he said.

But finally he made the decision and had his name put on a waiting list. It wasn't long before a small crew of men came and marked the trees to be cut. I felt sick inside as I looked at healthy oak trees and straight pines with criminal looking yellow spots painted on their trunks. At least our sycamore at the foot of the garden was not in the path.

The trees were cut and sold for timber, leaving a wide, ugly, stumpy avenue. And it stayed that way for months and months, the stumps sending up ragged sprouts, trying to reforest the land. "The die has been cast," Mamma said. "Now I wish they would come on." Daddy slammed his helmet down on the breakfast table in utter exasperation sometimes, having gone out early to see if the work was starting yet.

The day the electrical crew did come they almost scared me out of my skin. It had rained the day before, and I was on my way to Firewood Heights to see if there were any Boleta mushrooms, the kind that were so good to eat. Suzanne was going, too, but she had stopped to feed Crusoe first. Walking along in soggy leaves, swinging a lard bucket, I was talking out loud: "Oh, Sun, you're so pretty on the raindrops. I wish I could write a poem. If I could, I'd tell just how it feels to have sun-rainbows dancing at me from every side." I could say things talking out loud all alone that I would never say if someone were listening. When a twig broke near me I stopped dead in my tracks and, looking cautiously around, met the astonished gaze of a man in a khaki uniform. Then I saw the truck and other men with post-hole diggers. Consumed with burning embarrassment, I turned around slowly as the man finally said, "Good morning," and I heard him laugh as I took off running back to the house.

That had happened the day before. The men worked all day, and today they were to finish and we would be able to "throw the switch," the foreman told Charles. Charles had watched them closely after he found out they were there.

"Any minute now. They're almost through," said Suzanne coming back from peering out into the garage. She put her hands on Mamma's shoulders and jumped up and down ecstatically. "I'm going to be the first one to turn on the kitchen light," she said.

Betty and the children had come over to share our excitement. "Mom, could I have one of the kerosene lamps now that you don't need them anymore?" Betty enjoyed collecting antiques.

"Well, I think I better keep them all for awhile, Betty. You know, it's hard to believe I won't be needing them. I guess, after I've depended on them all my life, I can't believe I could suddenly do without them."

"Oh, Mom, you're really going to enjoy the electricity!" exclaimed Betty detecting a note of doubt. "Just think how nice it will be to have a light electric iron instead of those heavy iron ones you have to keep hot on the stove and handle with thick cloths."

"Yes. It will be good," Mamma said quietly.

I tried to picture the kitchen with a gleaming white electric stove instead of our black woodburning one with its white enamel oven door and warming closet. Would there still be that prized seat behind the stove to come to on cold afternoons? Running towards the house, heart pounding, you'd yell out, "I have A-1-A on the seat behind the stove." A-1-As were not always honored. If you had the seat and had to go out to feed the chickens or fetch eggs, you'd say "I want my seat when I get back," and, according to our unwritten law, that meant it would be yours. But if perchance you forgot to say the words, then it was a lost seat, and you had to find a second best one on the bench, in the woodbox, or on the warming tank.

"Eula, they're ready to throw the switch," said Daddy coming down the corridor.

The next moment was magical. White light filled the kitchen. Even in daytime it made such a difference we stood blinking in amazement a minute before we went to see how all the other lights did. Suzanne got up in a chair to pull the string that would turn on the Hall light. The one in the kitchen had been on when the current reached it so she hadn't gotten to pull it as she had predicted. "Look, Mamma," she exclaimed, "you can see the timbers better."

Daddy had to lay down the law later that day: no switching of lights until nightfall. It was such fun to see them come on we might have worn out the switches the first week if he hadn't stopped us. How did Edison ever figure all this out, I wondered. Charles explained to me about negatives and positives, but all I really understood when he got through (though I nodded my head as if it were all clear) was that I was positively confused. Daddy's rhymed comment stuck with me better than the scientific explanation: "We can thank God for the mind of Edison, and use the progress he created with discretion."

That night in the kitchen as Mamma fried mushrooms and I stirred up some cornbread by her careful instructions, she confided in me. "I'm really happy about the electricity. I can never seem excited about things, though. I guess it just doesn't bubble out the way it does in some people."

"Like Jackie and Suzanne."

"Yes. But even though I don't jump up and down, wring my hands, toss a dish towel, or whatever, I'm still happy about it. Just look how much you can see. I never realized how shadowy kerosene lamps made everything."

"Did you say to put sugar in this?"

"Just a little. And oh, Honey, just *look* at all the dust and cobwebs. My goodness, I didn't know everything was so *dirty*!"

"Oh, Mamma..."

"Here, let me finish that. I heard Daddy calling. It's time for your grammar lesson."

"Can't I finish this first?"

"No, your daddy doesn't wait. You know that. My goodness, we're going to clean this house tomorrow. Every inch of it!"

Charles was already seated by the lampstand where we read our lessons out loud. Instead of the kerosene lamp, though, there was a neat fluorescent reading lamp fastened to the wall. Slipping into my chair, I looked to see what Charles's silent laughter was about. He was pointing hysterically towards Daddy's bed where I saw, not Daddy, but a fantastic barricade built of opened boxes.

"All right, children," came his deep voice from behind the boxes as if nothing were at all unusual, "let's continue our discussion of the verb *to be*. Brenda, give me an example of a sentence using the verb *to be*."

"The light is bright," I said, and Charles whispered sarcastically, "Wow! How original!"

Chapter Thirteen
Where There Abideth Faith...

The winter of 1959 was a hard one. Mamma had predicted it would be extra cold when she saw the abundant crop of acorns in the fall. She said the acorns were provided to keep the squirrels fat and saucy through a long winter.

Pinedale had a heavy snow right after Christmas. I went home with Ginger and Del to Windsor, South Carolina, after Christmas and was supposed to return on the bus. But the snow was so bad in Georgia that buses weren't running when it was time for me to go. Del and some of the boys from his church drove me home. Since there was never any snow in Windsor, the boys were eager to get out of the car at the first sight of it. My own excitement grew as we saw snow piled high along the road nearing Toccoa. There were children sledding in grocery boxes or whatever they could find to give them a good ride.

At Pinedale there was a whispered hush among the trees that stood darkly in the whiteness. We walked all the way in the lane and up the hill, amazed at the beauty of hemlocks wearing white mink and holly trees with ice-encased leaves. The boys had a snowball fight. As icy powder showered down my neck, I screamed and grabbed handfuls of snow to throw back, very glad to be included in the fight.

At Stone Gables the steps were a hill of snow which we had to go up and over to get back down to the door. Even the dear old iron knocker had a little drift of snow on top of it. Inside, we shook the snow off our coats, piled them in a chair, and went back to the kitchen where Mamma made hot cocoa and cheese toast. The kitchen light had to be on even in the middle of the day because, with snow banked halfway up the window, it was really dark.

We hadn't had that much snow since I could remember. Usually we had enough for one good snowball fight, a batch of snow ice cream, and maybe a trashy snowman or two. This was so much better, so much more exciting—unless you had to drive all the way back to Windsor before dark as Del did. He and the boys didn't linger long. I felt a warm pinkness as one of the boys said just before sliding down the steps, "Come to Windsor again." The pinkness deepened as, after a last wave, I turned back inside right into Daddy who was laughing down at me. "Well, well, Brandy Brew, got yourself a beau, did you?"

Stanley and Charles had gone into business for themselves that year. They rented a building across the highway from Pinedale in which they housed the "Double Eagle." It was a gas station and grocery store which had become so successful that they had hired a teenage girl to help in the store after school and on Saturdays. I wanted the job, to be able to see all the people coming and going, to ring up their sales on the register. But Daddy wouldn't hear of it. The boys could take care of themselves, could shield themselves from unseemly language which he was sure would abound wherever the "world" came by. But not we girls. He had to protect his girls.

Nevertheless, we often spent time at the Double Eagle waiting for the boys to eat a meal we had brought so we could carry the plates back. Suzanne and I were both used as legs for Daddy's messages, which he frequently sent the boys. So we did hear some of the interesting fish tales, the lively country "yarns," and even solos by a guitarist who frequented one of the store's three chairs.

Occasionally Daddy himself went down late in the evening after sundown. His step was so quick it was hard to keep up with him. He seemed as lively at seventy-two as he had at sixty when I could first clearly remember him, maybe even livelier. But Mamma was afraid for his life when he went to the Double Eagle. He would cross the highway in front of cars, not even noticing them until they blasted their horns at him.

"You've got to keep him at home," Stanley told her one day. "One car had to squeal to a near halt and Dad never realized it was because of him. He could have been killed, but he just came striding into the store grumbling about reckless, noisy drivers. I guess he didn't notice how everyone stared at him. You really must keep him home."

But keeping Daddy from doing anything he'd made up his mind to do was as completely impossible as it had always been. If he began to mention walking to the Double Eagle, Mamma suggested quickly that they walk to the south woods instead or she'd say, "The *Saturday Evening Post* came today. Let me read some to you." But it didn't always work.

Orman was often at Pinedale between speaking trips. He was living in Clarkesville, preparing to go to the Philippines as a missionary. It had been such an exciting day when he and his family moved "home" from a pastorate in Chicago. He'd been gone for so long (all my life) that it was simply unbelievable he and Margaret and their four children were now living in Clarkesville. And unbelievable that in March they would be leaving to board a ship and be gone for four years.

Orman asked me to do some typing for him, listing items as he packed them in great steel drums for shipping. I was proud of that job, getting a thrill out of being sort of a partner with a brother who had always seemed like a distant second father before. I could remember his reprimanding me when I was little for "showing off" and being unladylike with my stunts. Now I was working with him, laughing and joking with him, and the years between us seemed to squeeze together.

It was near the end of February when spring broke through the cold soil, shooting up pointed blades of narcissus and jonquils. Mamma said it was premature, that we'd have some more winter, that if the flowers bloomed too quickly, they'd get their faces pinched. Daddy listened to the weather news very carefully every night before making his decision concerning covering the gardenia bush with burlap bags or letting his prized young German shepherd named Chieftain sleep indoors. He really liked letting Chieftain sleep by his door or even by his bed, but was determined not to spoil him. Though Mamma said he might as well spoil him. The dog, a beautiful gray and black with alert, pointed ears, wouldn't let Daddy take a step on the place he didn't follow right along.

Daddy was consistently in a good mood those days, walking the floors with his hands behind his back as he told us stories about people he'd known. Or sometimes he talked as he stood upstairs using the balcony rail in part of his exercise routine. Or he talked as he stood in the kitchen door or sat on the stone seat. Except for the times when he broke into a whistle, he was talking—about the past, the present, and the future. He often recited poetry he'd memorized years before. His favorite seemed to be Kipling's "Recessional." he rumbled out the words like thunder or breakers crashing against a rocky coast, sometimes the whole poem, sometimes only a stanza.

"God of our fathers, known of old,
Lord of our far-flung battle-line,
Beneath whose awful Hand we hold
Dominion over palm and pine—
Lord God of Hosts, be with us yet,
Lest we forget—lest we forget!"

Daddy could find lines of that poem to fit almost any situation that arose. After a family gathering he'd say, "The tumult and the shouting dies, The Captains and the Kings depart:" When he turned off the radio having heard news of heinous crimes he'd quote: "Judge of the Nations, spare us yet, Lest we forget—lest we forget!"

He quoted poetry with such vigorous expression that I would never be able to hear the words without superimposing his voice.

"The Lord has given me three-score-years-and-ten," he'd say, "and even this extra time with a mind that can still memorize and a wife to read to me and listen to my old worn-out stories with the patience of Job himself."

I didn't like for him to talk about the three-score-years-and-ten because I didn't like to be reminded that there was a limit to life on earth. Three-score-years-and-ten might seem long at the beginning, but at the end they were still over just like an added hour before bedtime. Bedtime comes even though prolonged. I didn't want to think about things changing or stopping.

But change did come and quickly. It came in the form of another tornado. After that, life at Pinedale was never quite the same.

Charles came up to eat an early supper and left with a plate for Stanley who was at the Double Eagle. As Daddy watched him go down the vista, he called out, "Don't you want your raincoat, son? It might rain before you boys close."

But Charles squinted at the cloudy-bright sky and said, "No, sir—thank you."

Suzanne wanted me to help her feed the dogs. The air felt funny, not exactly like rain. One dog was missing, and we went around the house hunting him. Mamma called as we rounded the front of the house by the boxwood. She wanted us to get some pine cones from under the white pines in the grove. They made such nice kindling for starting a morning fire. But as we started across the front terrace she called sharply, "No, don't go! Come back, girls!"

A blanket of ugly yellow had dropped over trees, house, and all. It seemed to have smothered all sounds and stifled all movement. There was not even a hint that minutes before the sun had been shining and birds singing. We hurried in the west door, looking back at the weird change that had taken place. The pine cones still lay under tall straight quiet pines, and the dog we hadn't fed followed us in the door whimpering and holding his tail between his legs, pushing against us for extra assurance and affection.

Daddy stood in the middle of the Hall floor with a foreign air of indecision as if he were waiting for something. Mamma was at the foot of the stairs, a dish towel twisted in her hands.

"I wish Charles hadn't left so quickly," she said.

"But we didn't realize..." Daddy's words were obliterated by a horrible rushing sound that wiped out all other noise. The cat arched its back and went up the stairs in flying leaps. Suzanne went after it. Mamma grabbed at her arm to stop her, but only succeeded in ripping her sleeve. I ran after her to bring her back, knowing we should be in the cellar as before. The windows along the balcony bowed distinctly inward, an awesome sight. I screamed in panic, but couldn't hear my own voice. Only the horrible roar could be heard. Then I almost fell over Suzanne who was crouched at the head of the stairs with the cat in her arms.

As suddenly as it had come, the roaring ceased. As light began to replace the yellow-blackness, we saw Daddy coming towards us along the balcony. A shocked stillness reigned, punctuated by cracking, alien sounds and a few spattering raindrops hitting windows like afterthoughts.

The tornado that came when the folks were on their trip had done no damage to the house or near the house. We had had to search to find where the funnel had dipped down. This time there was no need to search. The damage was all around the house. The grove was a shambles of twisted trees, stark, jagged trunks, trees across each other, uprooted ones with loose earth still falling from fan-shaped root systems. One large pine lay across the terrace wall at the south end of the house. An oak in the corner by the house had helped to catch it and had thus shielded the roof which was damaged very little. The holly was whole, but a few feet away were unsightly tree tops split open, exposing white centers. The air was spiked with the scent of broken pine.

It was inconceivable that all this had happened while all we heard was one overpowering roar. One tree falling can sound like a clap of thunder and here were literally dozens! Suzanne and I wanted to walk along the terrace—that is, climb along its labyrinth of fallen trees with limbs jabbed in the ground. But Daddy cautioned us, "Those trees may not all be settled yet. Trunks might turn with you, trap you under them. Go down the other way and see about your brothers. Only—be very careful."

Daddy, who blew up about the little things, like someone's interrupting when he was talking, or leaving a tool out in the rain, or turning a book back on its binding, took tragedies calmly, usually planning repairs instantly. But as I looked back at him standing there on the front steps, I felt a desperate sadness inside, for, though calm, he looked completely beaten. He looked really old. He hadn't put on his helmet, and there was nothing to hide the drawn pallor of his face, the absence of sparkle in his eyes, the gray strands of hair usually neatly combed around his bald spot, now awry. He needed to cry, I guess. But he never cried about that or anything else. Mamma put a hand on his arm, and he drew her to him tightly.

Charles was fine. We met him in the lane. "You won't believe your eyes when you see the mess around the house," Suzanne told him.

"I'll believe it," he said. "I'm just glad I'm here to see it. I wasn't too sure I was going to be. By running like a leopard I got to the store just in time to lie down on the floor with Stan. We thought the place was coming in on us. He'll need some more supper. I lay on his plate."

Daddy had had trouble sleeping for years. Mamma often stayed up after we were all in bed reading to him to help him relax. But after the tornado he had a much harder time. I would sometimes wake in the night to hear him singing "Rock of ages, cleft for me, let me hide myself in thee" or "My faith looks up to thee, thou Lamb of Calvary." His voice was hearty and strong in the blackness of the night, softened not the least for those who were sleeping.

The bulk of the tornado clean-up work near the house was done by the time we had a going-away dinner for Orman and his family. Daddy had been able to do a lot of the work himself and seemed unusually cheerful, considering the circumstances. Mamma said, though, that in the night he would lie awake and wonder out loud why those trees, friends to him all his life, had been taken. Why couldn't it have been those in the south woods or on Firewood Heights? She told me this because I was old enough now to be a confidante and maybe to help me understand Daddy better, for he was most demanding, rapping out orders two or three at a time, with no patience to wait for their accomplishment.

The night came for our last dinner with Orman and Margaret. As usual for a family gathering, it was a big delicious dinner with everyone chattering merrily, we younger ones sitting on the stairs to eat, adults gathered around the table. Daddy and Orman were especially hearty, launching into great stories capped with roars of laughter.

After dinner we gathered in a semicircle around the north fireplace. Two big logs glowed and crackled on the andirons. Orman said, "Remember, Mom, that delicious goulash you used to make in the iron pot that swung out over the fire on this crane?"

"M-m-m, I can taste it now," said Ginger who had come for the occasion.

There was a murmur of small talk then, but the air was so impregnated with solemnity that it couldn't be broken with light comments about the weather, the current hemline of ladies' dresses, or even possible candidates for next year's presidential race.

Daddy cleared his throat. "We'll just sit here by the fire as we say our verses tonight. At this solemn occasion when we see our son and brother leave for a distant land, I would ask you all, down to little John Mark here, to remember these words from Paul the apostle, 'Whether therefore ye eat, or drink, or whatsoever ye do, do all to the glory of God.' My father was a preacher. I am not, so I give you no sermon. I only ask that you do as I say, not as I've done. For I have made so many mistakes. This one admonition would stop so many mistakes before they even start, 'Do all for the glory of God.' The psalmist said, 'The heavens declare the glory of God and the firmament sheweth his handiwork.'"

Silence. Sparks flew up the chimney. Ginger's little Joel whimpered for a drink of water, Ginger shushed him and rocked him back and forth in her lap.

After Orman gave his verse selection, "As my Father hath sent me, even so send I you," each one down to John Mark gave theirs in turn. At the end of the Lord's Prayer, Daddy burst into spontaneous prayer and others followed him. The firelight shone softly on glistening, tear-wet cheeks when we raised our heads.

Daddy's song selection was "When the Roll is Called up Yonder." I was so proud of being able to play a little on the piano given me the fall before. But the occasion was so solemn, my hands shook with apprehension and I played as many wrong notes as right ones. The final strains of the chorus seemed to tickle the open beams way above us and tremble down the shiny stair rail: "When the roll is called up yon-DER, When the roll is called up yonder, I'll be there." It wasn't until later that year that I really thought about what that song said.

Tommy had learned to play a harmonica, and Mamma asked him to play "Jesus Loves Me." Then Margaret and Orman sang their new theme song, "Unto these hills around do I lift up my longing eyes." As they sat down, Margaret said, "You know, I don't feel you're my mother- and father-in-law. I think of you as my mother- and father-in-love."

Joel whimpered for water again and Ginger tiptoed across the slates.

Firelight showed me a mischievous twinkle in Charles's eyes. Though practically grown now, almost nineteen, he did still like to pull pranks. Whenever he got a chance, when no one else was looking, he pointed to the fire. I could see a bright coal center with red castles among the ashes, but I didn't know what he was really pointing at until the explosion came. It was such a loud cannon-like boom it put everyone into momentary confusion, scared Joe and Joel nearly out of their wits, and made the cat run sideways to the other end of the room where she stood in the shadow of a chair, her back arched, her eyes round and glowing.

Charles had put a joint of bamboo cane in the fire, much to the delight of Tommy who was the first to decide it was funny and burst into laughter. Orman, like the rest, began to laugh as the shock wore off. He was reminded of some other practical joke he'd endured and told us about it. The pain of farewells was eased by the humor thrown in.

ε▲ ε▲ ε▲

Orman had been gone only a few days when I waked one morning to hear Daddy talking to Charles in the next room. "I burned myself a little this morning. It doesn't seem too bad. I just sat down on the heater. Couldn't keep my balance. I think I tripped over something, but I haven't figured out what. Come on down soon, Charlie Boy, Mother has breakfast about ready."

He sounded so calm and unhurt that I didn't really think too much about it. Snuggling down under the covers, I took one last little nap before Suzanne began punching me. "It's time to get up, Goose. The sun is shining!"

Daddy didn't sit much that day. He walked and talked around the house, seeming most cheerful. Mamma asked him several times if she shouldn't call the doctor, but he always said, "No, no, it's only a little burn. There's no need for that." He stood often in the kitchen door, hands behind him talking about how much timber the tornado-stricken trees made, about the success of the Double Eagle, and about his mother with her daintiness and charm. He told about the time when someone had shot into his old home in Ducktown, Tennessee, and how courageous his mother and Aunt Dee had been. He bragged, too, on his own bravery as a small child.

Late in the afternoon as the sun began to drop behind the trees making orange halos around them, Daddy went to bed "to rest a little." Mamma had a crease of worry on her forehead as she came back to help me finish supper. "He really isn't well," she said. "I don't dare call a doctor if he doesn't want one, though. The doctor wouldn't have a chance to help him, he's so stubborn."

"Is the burn—that bad?"

"It's very bad. And I'm afraid that's not all. He keeps saying he tripped over something this morning, but—there's not a thing there to trip him."

I felt as if I had been shaken out of a cocoon where all was cheerfulness and peace into a world of foreboding danger. It had been such a beautiful day. If the burns were so bad, how had Daddy been able to walk around all day so relaxed and happy and teach us our lessons as if he enjoyed it?

I was frying pork chops, and Mamma was making some biscuits when suddenly she washed her hands and started towards the study, drying them on her apron as she went. I hadn't heard anything except the frying, sputtering pork chops. She came back and took the turning fork from me.

"We've got to get a doctor. Daddy's in pain now. Go to the Double Eagle and use the phone. Call Dr. Lumsden."

"Not Dr. Garrison?"

"Honey, Dr. Garrison is too old to make house calls now. Call Dr. Lumsden. And do hurry!"

It was almost dark then. There was only a faint seashell pink over the pine-speared place where the sun had disappeared. I sped down the vista. It was like literally running into the night, for down in the valley night had already fallen. All I could see were faint outlines of tree stems and the dark gables of the studio and of the cottage. As I spurted into the driveway, though, the sand was luminous as if God were making sure I could see the path.

As I rounded the spring bend, there was a terrific racket of dogs barking and growling not far across the brook on the ridge side. My heart thudded with new fear. When dogs barked like that it was because someone was with them, urging them, hunting with them. I set my eyes on the white-sand outline of the lane and ran even faster past the old entrance wall where a convict or a panther might easily hide, around the lime hedge curve, and across the bridge, very quickly in case something were under it. Maybe a sixteen-year-old should have overcome such fears, but I was at least determined to outrun them, and all my racing for years back did help out.

Finally I dashed past the vine-grown waiting-wall and reached the highway. The pairs of car lights rushing past seemed threatening, yet, on the other hand, comforting. A car would soon bring Dr. Lumsden to help Daddy.

As soon as I could get my breath, I dialed Dr. Lumsden's number. This was no time to be shy about using the phone. Stanley and Charles were both busy selling groceries and gas. I had to do it. My hand shook as I stood there listening to the ring in the telephone, wondering if I'd be able to hear above my heartbeat when someone answered. It rang four times, then finally a friendly lady's voice said "Hello."

Dr. Lumsden wasn't home, his wife said. She would send him out just as soon as he got in. There was nothing more to say. He had to be there, but he wasn't, so we would have to wait.

"Tell him to hurry, please," I said, trying to keep my voice steady. "My daddy's burn is really very bad."

Stanley left the station business with Charles and walked with me back to the house on the pretense of getting their supper.

"Your hand is as cold as ice," he said.

"The dogs scared me."

"What dogs?"

"A whole pack of them, running down the ridge towards the brook."

"Well, they must be gone now. I don't hear anything. Is Dad really that sick? Did he ask for the doctor?"

"Mamma sent for the doctor. I think Daddy agreed, though. He's hurting pretty bad, she said. I hope he didn't hear those dogs. It would worry him if he thought someone were hunting."

It was two hours before the doctor came. Two long, painful hours. Daddy had begun to realize that he had not tripped over anything that morning. He had just fallen because of momentary paralysis. Partial paralysis had kept him comfortable all day long so that he hadn't felt the pain from the burn.

Now it was a searing fire in a large area on his back.

Dr. Lumsden was cheerful, but evasive. He would not be pinned down to any definite prognosis. Mamma was to let him know the next morning how Daddy was. He had given him a shot to help him rest and told Mamma to keep a close watch. Better still, he should be in the hospital.

"No," Mamma said firmly. "I promised him I would not take him to the hospital. We will take care of him here."

Daddy never got up again on his own. Dr. Lumsden and the other doctors who attended him said he was having small strokes, one right after another. Ginger came with two-year-old Joel to help us take care of Daddy. It was a full-time job keeping his burns dressed, his medicine administered, feeding him what little he could eat, and most of all, keeping him happy. He wanted somebody to read to him almost constantly. I can remember reading when I was so sleepy my tongue seemed swollen and my eyes jumped from line to line. Sometimes he seemed sound asleep so I would stop to take a little cat nap, but he roused immediately when my voice stopped and responded to the last sentence I'd read.

Mamma called all the children in the States, but she worried about getting in touch with Orman and Brantley. Orman would not have even reached Guam yet, the first port where his ship was to dock. Brantley was on the other side of the world in Japan. It would be so hard on both of them to know how sick Dad was and not be able to come see him. Daddy would be all right, anyway. The strokes would stop and he would recover rapidly, as he always did. Daddy would be well, and there would have been no need to frighten them. Mamma would just tell them all about it in a long letter when Dad began to get better.

I never doubted that Daddy would get well. I talked with the others in phrases like, "If he doesn't make it..." "What will Mamma do?" "Daddy's woodpile...going down...will he make one next winter?" But in my heart I believed that Daddy was indestructible—like a piece of his granite or flint stone, like a river that always has somewhere to go, like a mountain with its roots on bedrock.

On April 11, Pat and David came for the weekend. It was their own Eric's second birthday. Daddy's mind had begun to cloud. He recognized Pat part of the time just as he did the rest of us. But at times he seemed to drift faraway, his eyes taking on a "who-are-you?" look. He would ask for his ax so he could chop some wood, or he would demand his pants so he could "get out of here." Yet he couldn't even raise up on his elbow.

While Pat was taking her turn sitting with Daddy, Eric cuddled in her lap, Daddy began hallucinating, his eyes seeing things that were not there, his hands making strange little motions in the air. Eric shivered in Pat's lap, she told us later, and then whispered, " 'et's git along outa here, Mommy."

It started raining while Pat and David were home, a flooding, drenching, soupy rain. It was Easter Sunday. David and I went to church at the high school auditorium. Our church sanctuary was being remodeled. It seemed as if everything were turning upside down and getting all mixed up. It was as if I were in a ship on a stormy sea. Even church was not right in a strange place with noisy folding chairs and a hollow sound when the preacher talked. The few people who had dared to wear Easter hats looked unreal, like Christmas lights in July.

In my Sunday school class, I asked the other girls and my teacher to pray for Daddy and choked on the last word, hunting desperately for a tissue. Jean handed me one, and no one said anything for a minute. Then the teacher said quietly, "We certainly will. And we know God will answer in the best way."

Daddy did seem to improve. Even the doctors (Dr. Hodges was now coming part of the time and consulting with Dr. Lumsden) said he was better. There were fewer strokes and, though there was some brain damage, he could possibly live for months, even years. It was a struggle for Pat deciding what to do. Lorna was school age, Pat had her own teaching job, and, of

course, David would have to return to his work at Union Carbide. But should she get a substitute teacher and stay at Pinedale? But—the doctors said Dad might even live for years. Finally all the Pecks left and, with everything so somber and dreary, I'm not sure anyone waved to them when their car passed the pond view.

The house continued to hold a hush of sickness and to smell of medicine and burns that would not heal. The hours were long and tiring for everyone, but especially for Mamma who would only let us take her place at Daddy's side by spells. When someone else was with Daddy, then Mamma worked like a Trojan in the kitchen or with laundry, refusing to rest.

Entering Daddy's room always meant stepping over or around his dog Chieftain who kept guard at the door waiting for his master to take him on one of those long walks. Suzanne tried to coax him away and John ordered him out, but at the first opportunity he was a silver and black rug again before the door.

Rain kept up a steady drum beat on the roof. Would it always, always be raining from now on?

We began to get silly with the strain. As we ate we shared some of the funny things Daddy said. Mamma was never with us when we were eating. I don't know how she got along, but I can't remember her eating at all. If she'd been with us we might not have laughed so hysterically about Daddy's saying to her, "Woman, give me my pants."

Ginger said Daddy interrupted her reading once to admonish her, "Take good care of your little fellow, the Little Prophet (Joel). Someone may try to take him someday." He'd also told her, "I've trusted the Lord every day. When each new baby was born He always provided." And then one day, "I see a man with a white beard beckoning me to come on over." Another day, in a disappointed voice, "I thought they would have come for me by now."

John came often, too, sometimes just to stand by Dad's bed a few minutes, sometimes to get in more wet wood to dry by the heater, or to bring more hospital supplies.

On April 18, I heard Mamma talking with Dr. Lumsden in the breakfast room. "It would be so much easier on you if he were in the hospital," Dr. Lumsden said.

"Is there anything you can do to save him there that you aren't doing here?"

I listened for the doctor's answer which was slow in coming.

"We could only keep him for a few more hours."

"Then he will stay here," Mamma said decisively. "I promised him. He wanted to stay at home so badly. I can do that for him."

Dr. Lumsden laid his hand on her arm, then turned to walk across the Hall, his black bag in hand. "Don't hesitate to call me—anytime," he said from the door. Mamma didn't see me standing close by as she pulled a handkerchief from her dress, wiped her eyes quickly, then slipped back in the study, closing the door behind her.

As we took our turns that day with Daddy, Mamma remained also, only leaving for absolute necessities. He didn't know any of us now. He seemed so strange with glucose tubing attached, lying so quietly in that borrowed hospital bed so much higher than our chairs. We wondered why he kept lifting his right hand in the air and making stroking motions with a faraway look in his eyes. Mamma said he was painting.

It was still raining. The driveway was almost impassable. Around every heater was a little circle of chairs, their backs hung with wet clothes trying to dry. Little Joel wanted so to go out to play and, even though we helped her, Ginger still looked worn and tired. She was five months pregnant. "I guess Daddy won't see my baby," she said. "Sure he will," I said confidently. "He's going to get well, I tell you."

The day was dismal and dark. Mamma was trying again to decide whether to wire the children and what she would say. She so wanted to protect them from unnecessary pain. It all seemed too great a decision to make as physically and mentally drained as she was. It had been three weeks now since Daddy burned himself.

We were eating tomato soup for supper. John was in the study with Mamma. Betty was trying to cheer us up which she could nearly always do. It was Saturday night, time for polishing shoes, studying Sunday school lessons, just about time for Daddy's favorite newscast.

Someone had just told a joke. I was trying not to laugh too hard with a mouthful of tomato soup and crackers. Mamma came out in the breakfast room and every giggle, every spoon rattle hushed instantly. "Come, children, all of you. Come quickly," she said. Stanley rushed out the door unbidden to go for Dr. Lumsden, but it was all over when they returned.

The next hours are a jumble in my mind—like a collage of scenes, crystal clear in spots, fuzzy and pain-erased in others.

There's the old cupboard where I leaned and cried until I felt sick, saying over and over, "Why, God? Why my Daddy? I wasn't ready for him to go. I'm only sixteen!"

There is John and Betty's house, neat and peaceful, where we took midnight baths while the mortician was at our house. There is the hearse, so big, so black, so ugly sitting in front of our own stone steps—impossible that it could be there. It should be out on the highway going to someone else's house. It didn't belong here. Death never happened here.

Another picture is of my trip with Del to Atlanta's airport to meet Jackie arriving from her home in Cambridge, Massachusetts, and my first sight of her coming towards us, her face so stoically set and white in the early dawn of Sunday morning. We talked about her two-year-old Sabrina's cute sayings on the way home and avoided even thinking about her reason for being there—until we had to.

There are the return cablegrams from Orman and Brantley, heartache in their every word.

I can still see Aunt Maggie making a fire in our cookstove. (Daddy hadn't been able to buy an electric range yet.) She seemed to know exactly what she was doing as if it were her own kitchen.

One of the distressing scenes is of dozens of cars spinning in the mud trying to get up the hill that rainy Sunday and parking all over precious spots. Daddy would have been so shocked and hurt to see the myrtle and grass torn up. But Daddy couldn't mind anymore.

All that food! A soft place began to grow inside my hard sorrow because people really cared so much. They came. They brought food. They sent flowers. They cared. There wasn't anything that could be said that would make Daddy be alive again and that was what I wanted. I wanted to wake up and know that this was all a nightmare and that he would be teaching history on Monday and supervising a weed pulling. No, friends couldn't wipe away our sorrows, but they could share it. And they did.

The funeral was on Monday. Just as Mamma had refused to take Daddy to the hospital unless it would really help him, so she refused to take him to the funeral home or church for the final service. She said he wanted it to be at home and at home it would be.

The sun came out and the sky was clear, swept clean of dreary rain clouds as family and friends filled the Hall, more people than it had ever held before.

Someone was playing our piano. It needed tuning, but we had put off having it done, not thinking of its being used for a funeral. Some notes were flat and some wouldn't play at all. And the right pedal squeaked. But the words to familiar hymns played through our minds, words we'd heard Dad sing in the dark of many nights: "When the trumpet of the Lord shall sound, and time shall be no more..."; "Abide with me, fast falls the eventide..."; "Rock of ages, cleft for me, let me hide myself in thee..."

The casket stood in the corner by Mamma's desk, not far from the big fireplace. The casket was there, but my Daddy couldn't be. As Preacher Brown exhorted, I sat streamy-faced, holding tightly to a completely soaked handkerchief. Out the north window I could see the branches of a dogwood tree swaying gently in the breeze. Blooms were just about to burst open. "I will lift up mine eyes unto the hills, from whence cometh my help. My help cometh from the Lord, who made heaven and earth," Preacher Brown read from Psalm 121, one of Daddy's favorite passages.

I looked around. We were all in this together. There was so much comfort in that. Silent tears washed the faces of several sisters and brothers and their spouses, others stared down at their hands or out a window. Suzanne held tightly to my hand. In front of me, Mamma sat beside Stanley, her hair neat and beautifully coiled on the back of her head. She had on a new black dress chosen for her by Pat that morning. Now she glanced anxiously at the door. We knew she was still hoping Rev. Johnson would walk in. He'd said he would come to assist with Daddy's funeral. Daddy had thought so much of him, had enjoyed talking with many preachers, but the young Rev. Johnson was a favorite, so Mamma had been bold enough to call him. But he lived now in south Georgia and must not have been able to come, after all.

"When I consider thy heavens, the work of thy fingers..."

Tears fell afresh. Daddy should be saying those words, Daddy walking under the pines. Were there trees in heaven? Was it spring there, too?

As we walked behind the pallbearers up Tulip Hill to the grave so carefully chosen, Mamma was close beside me. "Look at the forget-me-nots," she whispered. Mingled in green grass were thousands of tiny blue and white flowers as if freshly sprinkled there just for us. Birds sang joyously about us. The sky was shimmery blue with tufts of white clouds separating into smaller fluffs. "God gives us the tears, honey," Mamma was saying. "He knows we need them. When we don't need them anymore, he will wipe them away. Imagine! Daddy can see to paint now all he wants to."

When we were almost to the top of the hill Mamma turned to look behind her and I heard a little gasp of relief. There came Rev. and Mrs. Johnson through the grass and forget-me-nots. Their coming was in itself a gift to all of us and his words at the graveside service were very comforting. "We wanted to come earlier, but couldn't," he explained to Mamma at the house afterwards. We talked about old times and he affectionately recalled some of his long talks with Daddy. "He was someone who didn't just spout off an answer to my questions, but dipped deep into the well." I was eager to hear how Ruthie was and her mother showed me a picture. Before they left we all had a big laugh over some remembered episode, maybe about Charles and the tractor salesman. The laughter was good. Knowing it was okay to laugh was very good.

It was the next day when we realized Chieftain had disappeared. We hunted for him in the south woods, all the way to Sentinel Springs, along the ridge, everywhere, but no one could find him. Ray Nicholson scoured the neighborhood looking for Chieftain, but had to report with a shake of his head and his usually bright smile barely glimmering that Chieftain was nowhere about. Chieftain never came home. Humans can cry, rationalize, receive God's comfort when a loved one leaves so permanently. What can a devoted dog do?

It was much later, after Stanley had left to go to Seattle, Washington, to a new job, after we had supposedly "adjusted" to our loss, that we started hearing a roar in the north fireplace. Mamma said there was some explanation for it, but she didn't know what it was. Why had we never noticed it before? Every evening after supper when we sat in that end of the Hall reading, knitting, or writing letters, we heard the roar. It was like rolling thunder in the chimney and would last only a minute, then be all silent again.

"You know, we're going to have to work much harder now Daddy is gone," Mamma said one night. "We'll be taken over by weeds if we don't. Daddy kept things so neat just by working a little bit each morning and evening."

"With Stanley gone and Charles at the store all the time, how can we do it all?"

"We'll manage," she said, breaking off a thread.

I laid my book down and got up to play the piano. As I took hold of the stool to set it in place, the thunder-roar startled me. It seemed to shake even the stone chimney. We were stunned into an inanimate state like figures in a quiet music box—I with my hands gripping the piano stool, Mamma with a broken thread trailing from one hand, Suzanne ready to turn a page in her book with one finger of her left hand, her right laid fondly on a cat in her lap.

Mamma said thoughtfully, "It just seems as if that's Daddy's spirit talking to us, assuring us everything will be all right. I know it can't be, but..."

From then on the roar didn't bother me. God could do anything. He could let Daddy's spirit linger a little if it would help us, couldn't he? God who is big enough to care about every little thing could make a roar in a chimney at just the right time to comfort us. It was impossible to believe all at once that Daddy was gone. The house seemed to breathe of his presence, the stones he had sculpted and helped set in place, the giant timbers, the arches along the stairway, the translucent kitchen window with the mark of his chisel in the mortised arches.

Charles finally discovered that the sound was made by a flock of birds flying in and out of the top of the chimney. The dozens of little wings fluttering made a breathy, shaky roar. But I still believe God put them there at that particular time and tuned our ears to hear them right then for a purpose: to remind us that not only would we see Daddy again someday, but also that Daddy was truly living right then with Him.

ﻉﻩ ﻉﻩ ﻉﻩ

Since the first publishing of *Stone Gables* in 1978 our family has changed quite a bit. Mamma celebrated her 90th birthday in August, 1994. She took time from making peach pies, crocheting afghans and playing Scrabble to enjoy our gathering at Stone Gables with our covered dishes, our reminiscing, and all our children, or as many as could come. We are nearly a hundred folks now, counting thirty-three grandchildren, some with spouses, and twenty-nine great grandchildren, the newest little

Peck grandson only a few weeks old.

When we surround Mamma at one of these events she always looks around the Hall at our ever-enlarging circle and says with a shy, but proud smile, "Look what Dad and I started!"

We are grateful for what they started. We are thankful that even now we can come to Pinedale and be refreshed by the singing of birds high in the swaying trees, enjoy the rippled reflections of pines in the new pond Charles and Stanley made, and walk many new trails blazed by Charles's son Nathan. We are thankful we can take our children and grandchildren to Pinedale and cultivate in them an appreciation for little furry animals, flag-stones in Indian Spring, cucumber trees, fireflies at dusk, names carved in The Beech Tree, our log cabin schoolhouse, walking a footlog across Ramble Brook, and all those things.

But—Pinedale is more than a place. Pinedale is a helping hand, a shared laugh, a teary hug, a retreat from the mad rush, and a push to do our best. We are grateful that in the foundation of our beings was established a love for God, a respect of his creations, an ambition to share him with others, and a longing to be the people he wants us to be. And that's what Pinedale really is. Pinedale is people who care for us just as we are—wherever we are. And that it will always be. So we don't have to go to Pinedale to be a part of it. We've taken Pinedale and Stone Gables with us!

THE END

Brenda Knight Graham has written four other books, a series of three novels for children (Broadman, 1979, 1980, and 1981) and a historical romance, *Juliana of Clover Hill* (Zondervan, 1984; Guideposts, 1994). She and her husband Charles, a veterinarian, live in Cairo, Georgia. They have two grown children, William and Julie, as well as one granddaughter, Amanda. Brenda enjoys telling Bible stories to third and fourth graders at her church, playing harmonica, cross stitching, and walking with her Irish setter named Blakely.

John Kollock has illustrated over 30 books for different authors in addition to writing and illuminating his own works. As a regional artist in the mountains of Northeast Georgia he has been a personal friend of the Knight family for many years. It is with a special interest that he has approached this particular work. John and his wife Nancy live near Clarkesville, Georgia. Their three daughters are grown, but numerous pets including the charming Christmas letter writer cat Gwenevere keep the Kollock home lively.

SADDLEBACK Classics

Swiss Family Robinson

Johann Wyss

ADAPTED BY

Emily Hutchinson

SADDLEBACK
PUBLISHING·INC.

SADDLEBACK *Classics*

The Adventures
of Huckleberry Finn

The Adventures
of Tom Sawyer

The Call of the Wild

A Christmas Carol

The Count of Monte Cristo

Dr. Jekyll and Mr. Hyde

Dracula

Frankenstein

Great Expectations

Gulliver's Travels

The Hound of
the Baskervilles

The Hunchback
of Notre Dame

Jane Eyre

The Jungle Book

The Last of the Mohicans

The Man in the Iron Mask

Moby Dick

Oliver Twist

Pride and Prejudice

The Prince and
the Pauper

The Red Badge
of Courage

Robinson Crusoe

The Scarlet Letter

Swiss Family Robinson

A Tale of Two Cities

The Three Musketeers

The Time Machine

Treasure Island

The War of the Worlds

White Fang

Development and Production: Laurel Associates, Inc.
Cover and Interior Art: Black Eagle Productions

SADDLEBACK
PUBLISHING·INC.
Three Watson
Irvine, CA 92618-2767
E-Mail: info@sdlback.com
Website: www.sdlback.com

ISBN 1-56254-531-0

Printed in the United States of America
08 07 06 05 04 03   9 8 7 6 5 4 3 2 1